Sally Asher

111 Places in New Orleans That You Must Not Miss

emons:

This book is lovingly dedicated to Jennifer Kooken, who read every word, and to Glenn May, who bravely parked illegally many times, so I could take photographs. I love you both!

Bibliographical information of the Deutsche Nationalbibliothek
The Deutsche Nationalbibliothek lists this publication in the Deutsche Nationalbibliografie; detailed bibliographical data are available on the internet at http://dnb.d-nb.de.

Layout: Anja Sauerland, based on a design by Lübbeke | Naumann | Thoben
Edited by Tania Taylor
Maps: altancicek.design, www.altancicek.de
Basic cartographical information from Openstreetmap, © OpenStreetMap-Mitwirkende, ODbL
Printing und binding: sourc-e GmbH
Printed in Europe 2025
ISBN 978-3-7408-2350-4
Revised new edition, October 2025

Guidebooks for Locals & Experienced Travellers
Join us in uncovering new places around the world at www.111places.com

Foreword

New Orleans is a city that has been in an identity crisis many times over the course of its 300-year history. From French colony to Spanish colony to part of the United States, it was possible during that era to have lived under three different flags. And the city's beauty reflects a merging of cultures and traditions that created a place that lives, eats, and celebrates like no other city.

We bury above ground and dance at funerals. We throw parades for dogs, hats, and beans. We covet glittered Zulu coconuts and Muses shoes. We often have eight-foot reptiles within city limits. We have festivals celebrating almost every type of food, including Creole tomatoes, po'boys, beignets, and gumbo. We also have festivals for practically every kind of musical genre: Jazz Fest, Satchmo Summerfest, Praise Fest, Congo Square Rhythms Festival, Crescent City Blues & BBQ Fest… With over 130 festivals a year, New Orleans averages a festival every 2.8 days. And if you want to have your own parade? Fill out the proper permits and have one!

The World War II Museum, Bourbon Street, and swamp tours are favorites for a reason. Those are must-visits! But this book also spotlights the lesser-known places, to give you a broader, more enriching adventure.

The music of the city is everywhere if you listen: brass, jazz, Cajun, zydeco – yes, but also in the clip-clop of mules' hooves in the French Quarter, the rumbling of streetcars, and the crackling of oil when seafood hits the frying pan. It's in the tolling of the cathedral bells, the low moaning ship horns in the predawn hours, and the joyful voices of the people. New Orleans' magic is that its identity is always changing but it's always completely distinct and always welcoming. This book will give you an insight into what the real New Orleans has to offer, so you can find your own rhythm and magic.

111 Places

ate Chirp Cook

1 Aidan Gill for Men

An unapologetically male barbershop

Don't be surprised by the rows of meticulously arranged grooming products and accoutrements when you walk into one of Aidan Gill's barbershops in New Orleans, which are, to quote owner Gill, "unapologetically male." In the 1960s, Dublin native Gill noticed the steady disappearance of barbershops in favor of gender-neutral salons and became determined to save the centuries-old trade of barbering. He opened his first barbershop in New Orleans in 1990 as a sanctuary from the unisex salon and has been rightfully called the "King of the Barbershop" and the unequivocal leader of the barbershop resurgence.

His Magazine Street store is a testament to his passion. All the chairs are vintage Koken or Koch (often rescued and restored). His mirrors, cabinets, display cases, and bars all have a story (and a purpose). In the back room (the inner sanctum), customers enjoy Gill's signature 30–40 minute "Shave at the End of the Galaxy" while sipping some whiskey (or Guinness on tap – your choice), flipping through *Playboys*, admiring Gill's collection of cut-throat razors mounted gracefully (but masculinely) on the back wall, all while being treated to seven steaming towels pulled one by one through the course of your shave from a vintage 1910 towel-steaming machine.

Gill, often at great expense, purchases vintage barbershop memorabilia at auction to display in his shop, saving it from being used as a conversation piece in someone's bathroom. You will also find high-quality items handpicked by Gill himself: tubs of shaving cream, shaving brushes, cowhide razor strops for your straight razor, aftershave, and Gill's own line of shaving equipment. What you won't find at Aidan Gill is a female companion hovering by her male, dictating a haircut. Gill has a strict no-female policy and will politely (but firmly) ask them to leave. If they don't comply, the woman and the male customer are shown the door. Gill expertly blends tradition with technology in his shop, but what he doesn't blend is the sexes. "Unisex is a dead word in here," Gill states, true to form, very unapologetically.

Address 2026 Magazine Street, New Orleans, LA 70130 | **Hours** Mon–Wed, Fri & Sat 10am–6pm, Thu 10am–7pm, Sun noon–6pm | **Tip** Ladies, stroll a couple doors down to Trashy Diva, a local high-end clothing boutique (and line) inspired by everything vintage, which has a cult-like following. Trashy Diva Clothing Boutique (2048 Magazine Street); Lingerie Boutique (2050 Magazine Street); and Vintage Market (1920 Magazine Street).

2 Algiers Ferry

Second no more

For years, Algiers Point has been known as New Orleans' redheaded stepsister. Founded in 1719, one year after the French Quarter, it's the city's second oldest neighborhood. Ever since, the neighborhood has battled for centuries to overcome its second-tier status. And there is no reason for that. Algiers Point, in the truest sense, is a neighborhood. With multiple parks, restaurants, bars, and cafés, a close-knit community exists where residents call their neighbors and their dogs, cats, or even turkeys by their name. A ferry has connected the two neighborhoods since 1827. Today, the ferry is for pedestrians and bikers only and takes about 10 minutes to cross.

The architecture is stunning, with its colorful 19th-century Victorian cottages and Greek Revivals. The Algiers Courthouse, a brick, Italianate structure built in 1896, is a landmark. Bargeboard, LLC is an architectural salvage and antique store. Tout De Suite Café is a cheerful coffeehouse serving French and Cajun-inspired breakfasts and lunches. Barracuda Taco Stand and Margarita Garden is a lively outdoor restaurant with fresh food and ample seating. And Nighthawk Napoletana, right by the ferry landing, offers woodfired Neapolitan-style pizza pies and excellent wine and beer. The Old Point Bar is a classy dive bar with live music. Confetti Park, a whimsical playground for kids, has cypress trees, picnic tables, and its own local children's choir that performs around the city. Confetti Kids, a nonprofit organization for children, hosts multiple events each year, including a children's Mardi Gras Parade, Friendship Day Parade, Easter Egg Hunt, and Candyland Ball. Festivals occur year-round, including Wednesdays at the Point, which take place every Wednesday for eight weeks during the summer and feature outdoor concerts with food, drink, and art for sale.

The top attraction, however, is the Jazz Walk of Fame, which starts at a large statue of Louis Armstrong and consists of 17 stops along designated lampposts with biographical information on jazz legends, all along the unsurpassed view of the Mississippi River.

Address Next to the Audubon Aquarium at 1 Canal Street, New Orleans, LA 70130 | **Hours** Every 30 minutes Sun–Thu 6:15am–8:45pm, Fri & Sat until 10:45pm | **Tip** The Algiers Point Association offers multiple downloadable self-guided tours that cover its general history as well as even more local jazz landmarks.

3 Anne Rice's Grave

Queen of the undead

New Orleans native Anne Rice is best known for her series of novels the *Vampire Chronicles*. Born in 1941, Rice's family eventually moved to Texas where she met her future husband Stan in a high school journalism class. Upon the release of her first novel, *Interview with the Vampire*, in 1976, Rice focused on her professional writing career, and her work has sold over 150 million copies. Stan was also an accomplished poet and painter.

In 1988, the couple returned to New Orleans. After Stan died in 2002, Anne left New Orleans, eventually dying in December 2021. Rice's cultural mark on New Orleans has been incredible.

While many expect Rice's tomb to resemble a more Gothic style like her literature, it is actually a classical Greek Temple with doric columns. On the left side of the tomb are three of her husband's poems, including one dedicated to their daughter Michele (who died in 1972 right before the age of six and who was eventually reinterred in the tomb). It features a door with an iron scroll of roses and a stained-glass window with a basket of flowers and the words "May Perpetual Light Shine Upon Them O Lord."

Rice, who famously staged her own "funeral" in 1995, where she lay in a coffin and was driven to her book signing in a glass hearse, had a private burial. The year after her death, the Anne Rice Vampire Lestat Fan Club, which has hosted a Vampire Ball in New Orleans since 1989, held a second-line funeral for her in October 2022. An empty glass Victorian horse-drawn hearse with Rice's picture on the side and a single red rose inside passed by the Lafayette Cemetery and made its way to her former residence on 1239 First Street, where they had a moment of silence. Afterward, many mourners dressed as vampires, characters from her books, or in black-hooded cloaks, gathered at her tomb in Metairie Cemetery to pay their respects to the author. Visitors frequently leave flowers, notes, books, and even fangs on her tomb to show their reverence for the literary legacy of the "queen of the undead."

Address Lake Lawn Metairie Funeral Home, 5100 Pontchartrain Boulevard, New Orleans, LA 70124 | Hours Daily 7am–5pm | Tip One of Anne Rice's homes is the former St. Elizabeth's Orphanage at 1314 Napoleon, a 55,000-square-foot building of Second Empire Design. The building is now luxury condominiums and is still an architectural wonder.

4 Antoine's Restaurant

Secret wine cellar

In 1840, Antoine Alciatore opened Antoine's Restaurant in the French Quarter. Today, it is the oldest, most continually family-owned and operated restaurant in the United States. Classic dishes were invented or popularized here, particularly Oysters Rockefeller (so named because the first person to taste the dish asserted that it was as rich as Rockefeller) as well as Eggs Sardou, first served to actress Sarah Bernhardt. It was to be named "Divine Sarah," but she insisted playwright Victorien Sardou receive the honor.

Jules Alciatore, Antoine's son, is credited with the expansion of the restaurant in the 1890s, acquiring adjoining properties and building banquet halls, along with requiring a three-year training of the waitstaff.

Jules and the generations that followed him were also collectors. Jules meticulously saved letters, private menus, autographs, and newspaper clippings. His son Roy also kept everything, from receipts for his cigarettes to the china used for President Franklin Roosevelt's visit, to his collection of cookbooks, some of which date back to the 18th century. In 2019, cookbook writer Poppy Tooker worked with Antoine's and the Historic New Orleans Collection to gather and organize the collection. The result was 130 linear feet of historic materials.

Many of these items can be seen in Antoine's. Along the corridor outside the Mystery Room, aptly named because it is where cups of coffee were "mysteriously" filled with liquor during Prohibition, there are 17 cabinets holding antique beer steins and teacups, as well as ashtrays from China to Mexico to France to Michigan. The private dining rooms are all themed with memorabilia on display, but the pièce de résistance is the wine cellar. When the private rooms are not booked, guests can walk back and peek into the massive vault, which spans almost a city block and can hold 25,000 bottles of wine. If you can't get into Antoine's, around the corner from the restaurant on Royal Street is a small window where you can view the cellar, appealing to the oenophiles and history buffs alike.

Address 713 St. Louis Street, New Orleans, LA 70130 | **Hours** Tue & Wed 5–9pm, Thu–Sat & Mon 10:30am–2pm, 5–9pm, Sun 10:30am–2pm | **Tip** The Historic New Orleans Collection in the French Quarter houses the Antoine's Restaurant Collection, as well as multiple other collections pertaining to New Orleans history, a beautifully curated gift shop, and public bathrooms!

5 Audubon Labyrinth

A healing path

Audubon Park, a 340-acre park in the Uptown neighborhood, was named after naturalist John James Audubon. It's a fitting tribute since the park is an urban oasis with egrets, herons, and whistling ducks, plus over 2,000 trees, including southern magnolias, black tupelos and live oaks. But located in the southeast corner of the park is a mystical structure based on a design dating back thousands of years – a labyrinth. Labyrinths are found all over the world and are known for their healing energy and feelings of unity.

Husband-and-wife team Debi and Marty Kermeen created this one, and the couple found it especially challenging but ultimately rewarding. The truck loaded with bricks was en route to New Orleans when Hurricane Katrina struck. The Kermeens had to temporarily halt production, but upon resuming, the labyrinth took on an even more symbolic meaning as the city was rebuilding. It was the first original construction after Hurricane Katrina, and for many symbolized the resurrection of New Orleans.

The Audubon Labyrinth is modeled after the one in Chartres Cathedral in France, which was constructed around 1,200 years ago and has 11 circuits, the number of times a path passes between the center and the outside of the labyrinth. The Kermeens, who have built almost 75 labyrinths around the country and in Canada, always strive to connect the labyrinths together physically and spiritually. When they can, they take pieces of the labyrinths they are building and bury them at future labyrinth spots to link them. "Labyrinths give people a place to listen to that voice within," says Debi. While Marty was constructing the labyrinth, he also took items of significance from people who wished to have these articles buried beneath the structure, which only adds further significance to its enigmatic elements. As a further blessing, Marty was frequently the subject of curious entertainment for the Audubon Zoo elephants, who on their walk, would stand by the fence and oversee this mystical structure being built.

Address Audubon Park, midway between the St. Charles and Magazine Street side entrances, near East Drive, where Laurel Street dead-ends into the park | Tip The Kermeens also built the labyrinth in City Park by the Children's Museum. It is a seven-circuit labyrinth, smaller and not as complex so that, as Marty says, "children can stay focused."

6 Backstreet Cultural Museum

Culture runs deep

The Backstreet Cultural Museum is the ultimate expression of paying it forward. In the 1970s, New Orleans native Sylvester Francis was parading with the Gentlemen of Leisure Social Aid & Pleasure Club when a photographer took his picture and wanted to charge him $35 for his own photograph. To avoid this happening to anyone else, Francis bought a Super 8mm camera and a still camera and started documenting second-line parades, jazz funerals, and Carnival celebrations himself. For over 30 years, Francis documented more than 500 films and videotapes of the African American parading culture. For every photograph he took, he made two images, one for himself and one for the subject, free of charge.

Mardi Gras Indians evolved as a tribute to the Native Americans who sheltered and protected runaway enslaved individuals. They are known for the elaborate suits they only wear on Mardi Gras Day and the Sunday preceding or following St. Joseph's Day. These elaborately designed suits are sewn with thousands of beads, rhinestones, sequins, shells, and feathers, costing upwards of $10,000 to make and a year to create.

After witnessing a Mardi Gras Indian suit left to the elements – they are only allowed to wear the suit the year it is made – Francis started collecting the discarded suits from his fellow Indians. By the late 1980s, he had amassed an impressive collection. What started as a "mini museum" in his two-car garage in the "back streets" of the Treme neighborhood, has expanded into a nonprofit and a museum housing the largest collection of Mardi Gras Indian suits, as well as hundreds of hours of archival film, countless photographs, and other Mardi Gras memorabilia from many other social aid clubs and "gangs." The exhibit is constantly rotating different suits and artifacts. At any given time, there are approximately two dozen beaded suits on display. The museum recently expanded from two rooms to a third space upstairs. Since Francis passed in 2020, his daughter Dominique now runs the museum, and like her father, promises a "real, raw history" of New Orleans African American culture.

Address 1531 St. Philip Street, New Orleans, LA 70116 | Hours Tue–Sat 10am–4pm | Tip On Mardi Gras Day, multiple "gangs," tribes, and social aid and pleasure clubs gather at the Backstreet Museum to start their day.

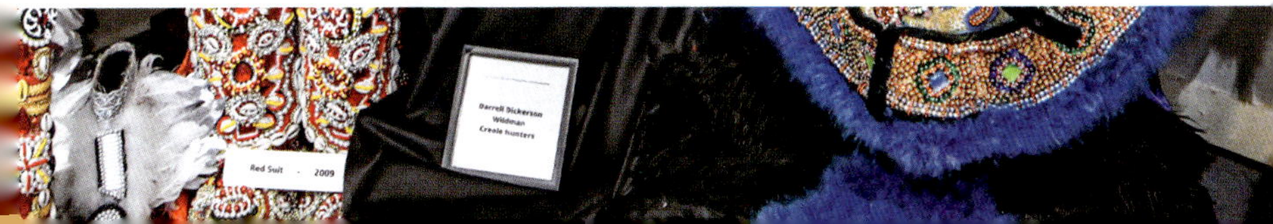

7 Bayou Sauvage

Experience wildlife off Bourbon Street

Bourbon Street has the reputation for being the wildest part of New Orleans, but located within the city limits is an Urban National Wildlife Refuge, Bayou Sauvage, which literally means "Wild Bayou." Pronounced "Bye-you So-vage," this 27,190-acre refuge was founded in 1990 and is only 15 minutes from the French Quarter, making it the largest urban national wildlife refuge in the United States. The refuge is one of the last remaining marsh areas adjacent to Lakes Pontchartrain and Borgne, also serving as protection for New Orleans, with most of it located inside massive levees to prevent storm surges and flooding. Many driving along I-10 in New Orleans East between the twin bridges that cross Lake Pontchartrain are unaware that they are driving through the hub of a wildlife refuge that is teeming with life.

Bayou Sauvage, bountiful in wildlife and recreational activities, contains a multitude of wildlife habitats including freshwater, brackish, and estuarine tidal marshes, canals, lagoons, lakes, cheniers (former beach fronts lined with trees), and bayous. There are sections of bottomland hardwood forest, old natural levee ridges with oak, and vibrant plant life, such as water hyacinths and lilies, lotus, black-eyed Susans, golden St. John's wort, coral honeysuckle, and zigzag irises. All this flora makes it a haven for wildlife. Almost 350 bird species can be found year-round, including white egrets, blue herons, woodpeckers, brown pelicans, osprey, and bald eagles. During the cooler months, Bayou Sauvage is home to thousands of migratory birds as a stopover on their way to warmer tropical regions. Also found here are white-tailed deer, otters, wild boars, raccoons, snakes (beware of the poisonous water moccasins), and the star attraction, alligators. While nature walks, hikes, and birding are easily accessible around the preserve, for those who wish to view the swamps and marshes more on eye level, there is a dedicated kayak, canoe, and paddleboard launch, but it is strictly BYOK (Bring Your Own Kayak).

Address 17160 Chef Menteur Highway, New Orleans, LA 70129 | Hours Daily during daylight hours | Tip Jean Lafitte National Historical Park and Preserve in nearby Marrero is named after pirate Jean Lafitte and has more than 26,000 acres of wild Louisiana wetlands.

8 Bevolo Gas & Electric

Modern antiques

Iconic copper gas lanterns line the French Quarter streets and create a romantic glow, casting soft shadows on the brightly colored shutters, elaborate wrought-iron balconies, and worn brick exteriors. In the early 19th century, gas lanterns supplied light to the French Quarter's streets. While most cities have replaced gas with electric lighting, the French Quarter has remained devoted to this cherished institution.

Bevolo Gas & Electric Lighting is a fourth-generation, family-owned business dating back to 1945 when Andrew Bevolo, Sr. revolutionized the production of gas lamps by utilizing a hand-riveting technique instead of soldering joints. Today, Bevolo lamps are found at many historic landmarks, such as The Cabildo, Jackson Square, and Brennan's Restaurant. While they have continued to evolve, Bevolo have kept their business extremely customized and personal. You cannot simply order online; they connect you with a lighting designer to help you choose from their 500-plus designs. All their products are manufactured in the French Quarter or in the greater New Orleans area. One of their locations allows you to observe the process.

The main business, on Royal Street, is an exquisite brick-exposed rectangular building that has entrances on both Royal Street and Exchange Alley. You are greeted at the Royal Street entrance with rows of gas lamps hanging on brick walls. In the middle is an open-air courtyard. Further back through the double French doors, craftsmen create copper frames on an old bowling alley floor repurposed as their worktable. Various tools, vintage memorabilia, and supplies line the walls. Tour groups, individuals, and families stroll through the space, pausing to watch these artists at work as they amiably answer questions and describe their process, creating a relaxed and intimate experience. "The historic cityscape of New Orleans – that ambiance and romantic feel we know and love," says Brittnee Ulmer, the company's brand manager, "is created here." The Bevolo family business continues to keep the flames of craftsmanship and personal service aglow.

Address 310 Royal Street, New Orleans, LA 70130 | Hours Mon–Sat 9am–5:30pm | Tip M.S. Rau in the French Quarter is one of the most respected fine art, antique, and jewelry galleries in the country. This 40,000-square-foot showroom is like an ever-changing museum.

9 Black Gold

One brave horse

The Fair Grounds Race Course is the nation's second-oldest racetrack, operating since 1872. It is known for its thoroughbred horse racetrack, racino, and for hosting the New Orleans Jazz & Heritage Festival. It also holds less traditional racing events like its Wiener Dog Races and Exotic Racing where jockeys ride animals such as camels, ostriches, and zebras. It is less famously known, however, as a horse graveyard of sorts.

In 1917, Rosa Magnet Hoots, a full-blooded Oklahoma Osage and the widow of Irish rancher Al Hoots, promised him on his deathbed to breed their mare Useeit, a racehorse with dubious pedigree. With a mixture of luck and grit, Rosa fulfilled her promise. The result was Black Gold, nicknamed for his sleek jet-black color and as a reference to the oil recently discovered in Oklahoma.

Black Gold was considered undersized but showed a winning resolve. His career started at the Fair Grounds in 1923 where he won nine races in 18 starts. The following year, Black Gold won the Louisiana Stakes by six lengths and followed up by winning Derby races in three other states.

In 1924, Rosa made history when she took her seat in one of the owner's boxes at Churchill Downs, only the second woman and the first Native American to do so. Black Gold won by half a length. It was the first time a woman had both bred and owned the winner. Sadly, at the end of 1924, Black Gold suffered a foot injury. Typically, Black Gold would have been put out to stud, but he was sterile. After some idle years, Black Gold returned. In 1928, he was back on the Fair Grounds Race Course. Sadly, Black Gold broke his leg during the run but, ever the determined spirit, finished the race on three legs. He died on the same track where he won his first race. The following day, flags were at half-staff and schoolchildren were let out to attend his burial in the infield. Today, an obelisk stands at the grave of this resolute and brave horse.

Address 1751 Gentilly Boulevard, New Orleans, LA 70119 | Hours Racing Office: 8am through the last race; Grandstands and Clubhouse open an hour before first race and close after end of last race | Tip Liuzza's by the Track, a casual Creole tavern by the racecourse that has gumbo and its signature BBQ shrimp po'boy, is the ultimate street party before and after each day of Jazz Fest.

10 Bottinelli Place

A son's tribute

On a one-block, dead-end of Canal Street between St. Patrick Cemetery No. 1 and Gates of Prayer Cemetery is an unusual building, even by New Orleans standards. On top of the three-story, brick building a re two identical Byzantine spires. At first glance, one would assume the spires are somehow related to the cemetery. They are not; they are a son's tribute to his beloved father and a testimonial to the city's architecture.

Teodoro Bottinelli was born in Brenno, Italy in 1886. He immigrated to New Orleans in the mid-1920s via Massachusetts. A talented sculptor, he made his mark with his friezes on many of the tombs in New Orleans. His most famous (and most controversial) contribution, however, was carving the bas-relief of Robert E. Lee's head at Stone Mountain, Georgia. Unfortunately, Bottinelli died from silicosis at the age of 46, the result of years of inhaling crystalline silica dust. He left his widow and two young children in dire straits. To earn extra money, son Teddy Bottinelli cleaned and weeded tombs, and his mother opened Quality Flower Shop out of the front room of her home. Over the years, the family bought more properties on the block. In 1978, at the family's request, City Council changed the name of the one-block street to Bottinelli Place. Teddy imported 200,000 quartz stones from Northern Italy and spent seven and a half months laying the stones out in a fan-like pattern to resemble the streets from his father's native country.

Teddy, who said he hated anything to go to waste, started taking salvaged items and adding them on to the brick building, including the spires, some windows, a cast-iron column, and cast-iron staircase from the former Temple Sinai. The arched windows came from the hayloft of the Old Dock Board stables, iron fences came from homes on St. Charles Avenue and are used throughout the block, and the mansard roof on one of the buildings is from the former St. Aloysius Brothers Home on Esplanade Avenue. The block, which appears as a mélange of styles, shows the passion of a preservationist and of a son.

Address Bottinelli Place is a one-block street that extends along the 4900 block of Canal Street | Hours Viewable from the outside only | Tip Teodoro Bottinelli's tomb in Metairie Cemetery is also a tribute to him, built decades after his death. The tomb features life-sized statues of him and his wife Emma. Bottinelli's sculpture shows him with his tools and posing with Robert E. Lee's head to immortalize his craft.

11 Boutique de Vampyre's Apothecary

A tasty time travel

Dining at the Boutique de Vampyre's Apothecary is not just a meal but an event. The exquisite attention to detail is apparent in this over-200-year-old French Quarter building. All five bathrooms have different themes: the Peacock, Mythical Creatures, Barbershop, Casket Girl, and Séance. The food and cocktail menu are impressive with its boudin-stuffed quail, Muffuletta Panini, and the "Fangria Blood Bag," but there are also multiple spaces to enjoy your food or drink.

The bar is made from 100-year-old cypress trees. The Flower Room has dried herbal flowers hanging from the ceiling. The Tree Room has, of course, a tree, exposed brick, mushrooms and moss in the dog friendly courtyard with a fairy fountain offers a menu for your four-legged friend and is guarded by a massive gargoyle named Horris.

The upstairs, where you are free to enjoy your cocktail, doesn't have service during the day but has a bartender at night and a separate drinks menu. The Casket Girl Room has the screen-used casket Vampire Bill Compton was killed in, from the *True Blood* series and has a separate séance room.

Additionally, there is always a psychic available from 11am to midnight to give tarot and tea readings and séances; a private Fang Room where you can make an appointment to have your own custom fangs made; and a private Chef's Table Séance Experience that includes champagne, a one-card reading, five-course meal, and an hour-and-fifteen-minute séance or an apothecary-themed magic show from Dr. Dalgo's Diabolical Delusions, which also has a regular Friday night show. A traditional English high tea is served on the last Sunday of every month and includes a tea reading and chocolate bats for dessert.

All of this, according to owner Marita Crandle, creates a magical environment for daywalkers and nightwalkers alike to travel back in time in ol' New Orleans.

Address 725 St. Peter Street, New Orleans, LA 70116 | Hours Daily 11am–2am | Tip Crandle also owns the Boutique du Vampyre and the Vampire Café, both in the French Quarter.

12 The Broad Theater

Indoor and outdoor entertainment

In 2016, the Broad Theater in Mid City opened its doors. Since then, this four-screen movie theater has not only become "the little movie theater that could" but a beloved local community hub. The historic building has transformed over its more than 100-year history from a former plumbing and heating warehouse to a boxing gym, law office, and even an oyster-processing facility. Owner and founder Brian Knighten works to keep the movie showings as broad as his theater's name. One week, the theater might be showing the latest Marvel Universe film alongside a black and white art house film, a foreign language film, and a classic romantic comedy.

While the Broad radiates the charm of an old-school movie theater, it has many modern and innovative touches. The concession stand is stocked with classic favorites like candy, popcorn, hot dogs, and nachos, but their ever-changing bar menu offers domestic and imported drinks, THC seltzers, and craft cocktails, including their spin on the classic New Orleans drinks, Pimm's Cup, Mint Julep, and the Sazerac. There is also a small pinball room located in the theater, thanks to the Mystic Krewe Pinball Parlor, a local social club that works more as a collective, meeting to play games, teach various classes, and collaborate on projects. Knighten works with many local nonprofit organizations who use the theater for fundraising.

The Broad also has its specialty nights, including $6 Tuesday where all movies, all day, are $6. Wednesdays are "Gap Tooth Cinema" where they show a specialty movie curated by filmmakers and artists from New Orleans and around the world.

Recently, Knighten expanded by adding the Broadside, a concert venue next door that has live outdoor music and movies, as well as an indoor event space that hosts everything from weddings to private parties, to hula hoop classes. Also located at the Broadside is Nikkei Izakaya, a casual Japanese pub-style restaurant where diners can eat in or take food outside to eat while they enjoy the latest event.

Address The Broad, 636 N. Broad Street, New Orleans, LA 70119; The Broadside, 600 N. Broad Street, New Orleans, LA 70119 | Hours The Broad is open seven days a week; hours vary | Tip The Prytania Theatre is a single-screen movie theatre in the Garden District; it is the oldest operating movie theatre in New Orleans and the last operating single-screen movie theatre in Louisiana.

13 Bucktown Marsh Walk

Birdwatching paradise

Located less than eight miles from the French Quarter, Bucktown is hailed by many as the ultimate seafood destination. It was originally clusters of cabins and fishing camps built on stilts over Lake Pontchartrain and along the 17th Street Canal. Its residents were primarily fishermen, and the area became known for its fishing and its fighting.

The history of Bucktown's name is debated, as some believe it is named after the "young bucks" coming to the area to find their "does," while others believe it is named after a specific man. Who that man is specifically is debatable, but they all share similar traits – they are nicknamed Buck, are tough, short-tempered, and possess enough swagger to have the area known as "Buck's Town." After the closure of the redlight district Storyville, many of its former denizens found their way to Bucktown, and since it was largely ignored by law enforcement during Prohibition, it became a hedonistic escape. While it wasn't vulnerable to convention, it was vulnerable to the weather and was severely damaged by hurricanes in 1915 and 1947. The lakefront levee was eventually raised, and most of the camps were eliminated, with the last of them removed in the 1980s. During Hurricane Katrina, the eastern floodwall failed, destroying houses in the Lakeview area. Now, to escape the bustle of city life, people venture to Bucktown for its fresh seafood and nature.

The Bucktown Marsh Boardwalk is a 3.4-acre man-made marsh that opened in 2020 as part of the Bucktown Harbor. Its 1,000-foot-long boardwalk includes benches, educational signs about the preserve, its plants, wildlife, and coastal ecosystem, and birdwatching stands to catch great blue herons, white egrets, black-bellied whistling ducks, yellow-crowned night herons, white ibises, and Louisiana's state bird, the brown pelican. The boardwalk lazily bends around a shoreline of marsh grasses and shrubs that help support the nearby levee system. Any time of the year offers a respite, but sunset is especially beautiful, as the boardwalk looks out west across Lake Pontchartrain.

Address 325 Metairie-Hammond Highway, Metairie, LA 70005 | Hours Open 24 hours | Tip Located nearby at 216 Metairie-Hammond Highway, R&O's Restaurant is a family-owned restaurant that specializes in fried seafood and New Orleans-style Italian specialties.

14 Bug Appetit

Crickets on the menu

For those who are afraid of creepy crawlers, the Audubon Insectarium will help you overcome your fears and quite possibly convert you into a bug lover by the end of your experience.

Formerly located in the U.S. Custom House, the Insectarium moved to the site of the Audubon Aquarium and reopened in June 2023. Although a part of the aquarium, the insectarium stands on its own legs (sometimes eight of them). Multiple exhibits exist throughout the space, including a live beehive, the Bait Shop, where people can touch insects, and the Butterfly Garden, where large colorful butterflies from Costa Rica and Ecuador surround you. The insectarium purchases chrysalises from farms as a way for people to generate money from maintaining healthy forests instead of destroying them.

The Bug Appetit, however, offers a totally different immersive experience. Many of the tables in the café are vivariums, enclosed areas for keeping and researching animals. One table is dedicated to silkworms, others to rhinoceros beetles, crickets, and tarantulas. The café is free, with enthusiastic staff handing out samples from a rotating menu. The most popular item is the Chocolate Chirp Cookie, with a roasted cricket on top. The "Beetledoodles" are their version of snickerdoodles, except they are made with mealworm, cheddar bacon crickets, and cool-ranch crickets. Their hummus, salsa, and mango chutney include ground-up and cooked insects. During Carnival season, they have Cricket King Cake, a cinnamon-filled king cake with roasted crickets inside and on top. "We want to introduce entomology as something perfectly normal to do," said Bradley Hiatt, the Lead Invertebrate Keeper. "We think of bugs as food." If you are worried about getting anything stuck in your teeth, not to worry. They "de-leg" all their crickets before cooking. According to Hiatt, most insects have a nutty flavor, but fried dragonflies taste more like fried soft-shell crab. The insects are all purchased from farms that raise them under strict FDA standards for human consumption. So do some good, eat a bug!

Address Located in the Audubon Aquarium, 1 Canal Street, New Orleans, LA 70130 | Hours Insectarium daily 10am–5pm; Bug Appetit daily 10:30am–4pm | Tip To get a better view of the Mississippi River, Vue Orleans is located atop the Four Seasons Hotel and offers a 360-degree panoramic view and interactive exhibits on the history and culture of New Orleans (ticket required).

15 Bywater Bakery

Inclusivity baked in

Buying a Chantilly cake from the Bywater Bakery is like hearing Frédéric Chopin play his nocturnes live. There is not much to beat it.

New York native Chaya Conrad graduated from the Culinary Institute of America and did her externship in New Orleans. She was the head of the Pastry Department for Whole Foods at Arabella Station when she created the Berry Chantilly Cake, a layered vanilla cake with Chantilly cream frosting and fresh berries. Today, it is sold nationwide. Uproar occurred in 2024 when they replaced berries with jam. The outrage was fierce, and Whole Foods returned to the original recipe.

In 2017, Conrad followed her dream with her husband Alton Osborn, a New Orleans native, former carnie, Merchant Marine, fashion designer, and world traveler, and opened the Bywater Bakery. Their "star," the Chantilly Cake, was followed by its culinary cousin, the Chantilly King Cake as well as traditional fare. They also, however, invented several fusion dishes. Osborn's grandmother's gumbo recipe has been transformed into a "breakfast gumbo," which is slathered on grits instead of rice. Their version of *Yaka mein*, a beef noodle soup known as "Old Sober" for curing hangovers, has a fried egg instead of a boiled egg.

The owners live by the creed that food brings people together, and their goal to bring the community together has succeeded with "reward programs" for children with good report cards, cupcake fundraisers for local band uniforms, and a welcoming place for all. Osborn, who now adheres to morning hours, missed live music and decided to host outdoor music performances (weather permitting) on the weekends. He refers to his wife as the "baker" and him as the "vibe," and books musicians of various styles, genres, and backgrounds.

The menu changes, but the Chantilly cake is still the pastry prima donna. This signature cake is now nationally famous, but so local. In fact, it's a great food metaphor for the bakery and the namesake neighborhood.... Layered, colorful, and full of delicious surprises.

Address 3624 Dauphine Street, New Orleans, LA 70117 | **Hours** Thu–Sun 8am–3pm | **Tip** New Orleanians will only eat king cakes during Carnival, January 6 (Twelfth Night) until Mardi Gras Day. Do not expect to find any king cakes after Lent, for natives consider it very bad luck to consume one after Carnival.

16 Cascade Stables

Horses and the city

The only stable located in the middle of the city, Cascade Stables has been in operation under owner Barbe Smith since 1981. Smith, who grew up riding at the stables, took it over when the former owners retired, and renamed it. The four-acre facility is home to about 70 horses, including those that are privately stabled, a collection of ducks, a donkey named Matza, his best friend – a miniature horse named Sweet Pea – and a goat named Ivan after Ivan the Terrible, for his penchant for eating Smith's paperwork.

The stable offers boarding, riding lessons, and competitive training, but one of its most popular experiences is the trail ride under the live oaks of Audubon Park. The trail horses, according to Smith, are "bomb-proof," as they often deal with dogs, kids, cars, etc. The horses, which only walk, are well trained for both the novice who has never been on a horse and the most seasoned rider. The ride takes about 45 to 60 minutes, crosses Magazine Street, passes by Tulane and Loyola Universities, Audubon Place, the Meditation Garden, a section of the golf course, and part of the Audubon Zoo.

Smith and her team also train the horses for the riding lieutenants in Mardi Gras parades, such as Rex, Proteus, Bacchus, and Iris. In December of each year, Smith purchases about 40 horses, and her "lesson kids" train them for the parades. If the trail horses are bomb proof, the parade horses are rocket proof as they endure screaming crowds, marching bands, flashing lights, and thrown beads and trinkets. Afterward, some of the horses are kept as trail riders and others find homes under the Humane Society's Adoption Program.

This family-run operation also gives back to the community by partnering with nonprofits such as Son of a Saint, which mentors hundreds of fatherless young men in New Orleans, and the Chartwell Center, which works with individuals with autism spectrum disorder and provides free riding lessons. Cascade Stables is a charming haven for the horses and a welcome escape from city life for the riders.

Address 700 East Drive, New Orleans, LA 70118 | **Hours** Trail rides are available Fri–Sun 10am–4pm, scheduled by appointment on the hour | **Tip** After the ride, visit Creole Creamery, an ice cream store that has classic and local favorites. Take the "Tchoupitoulas Challenge" – eight scoops of ice cream, your choice of eight toppings, all served with whipped cream, cherries, and wafers. Eat the whole sundae, and you will be immortalized on their Hall of Fame plaque.

17 Claiborne Corridor

Cultural innovation

In the 19th century until the mid-20th century, Claiborne Avenue was a thriving Black community. Hundreds of oak trees lined the street, setting a record in the country for having the longest single row of oak trees. The wide grassy neutral ground held sporting events such as football and baseball, and families gathered for picnics and second lines. The streets were also lined with Black-owned businesses including insurance companies, grocery stores, pharmacies, photo studios, and theaters. It was considered one of the "grand avenues" of the city, like St. Charles or Esplanade Avenues.

In the 1960s, preservationists successfully fought against having an interstate built through the French Quarter, but the Claiborne residents lacked the resources and political power, and when construction started on Interstate 10 in 1966, the effects were catastrophic. The majestic oak trees were torn down, and approximately 500 homes and 326 Black-owned businesses were destroyed. The once-vibrant greenspace and thriving community became a concrete desert. For years, many residents watched helplessly as one of the oldest African American neighborhoods rapidly declined.

Resourcefulness, however, still existed, and residents started using the space "under the bridge" as a gathering place for parades, krewe dance rehearsals, marching band practice, crawfish boils, and barbecues. Recently, thanks to civic and cultural leaders, multiple grants, and work from various nonprofits, the space is experiencing a rebirth. With assistance from the Arts Council of New Orleans, murals of legendary cultural bearers of the city were painted down the corridor. The space is being reimagined as a market and gathering place for art, crafts, and produce as well as social services, special events, and community activities. This resident-driven effort is working toward making "under the bridge" a place that serves and enhances the neighborhood. In December 2024, a historical marker was unveiled with much fanfare, honoring the spot as a landscape of Black entrepreneurship.

Address North Claiborne Avenue from Elysian Fields to Orleans Avenue, New Orleans, LA 70116 | Tip All the medians in New Orleans are called neutral grounds. The term derives from the 19th century when the middle section of Canal Street, which divided the French Creoles and the Anglo-Americans, was a "neutral ground" to meet, eat, and shop. The name stuck.

18 Congo Square

Ancestral worship

Congo Square, located right outside the French Quarter in Louis Armstrong Park, is one of the most sacred and historic areas in New Orleans. For more than 1,000 years before the French arrived in 1699, several Native American tribes populated the land. By the early 1800s, in an area where the natives once freely roamed, the square became a cruel paradox, the only place where enslaved people and free people of color could gather. Records show that these individuals danced, drummed, and sang, these forms of expression often taking on religious meaning. These African demonstrations gradually evolved into the Black Indian traditions, Second Line, and early New Orleans jazz.

In 1993, the square was listed in the National Register of Historic Places and later received a historic marker acknowledging it as "Congo Square," but what most people didn't know was that its official name was Beauregard Square, after Confederate General P. G. T. Beauregard. It wasn't until 2011 when author and historian Freddi Williams Evan sent a presentation on the history of the Square to the City Council that they officially named it Congo Square.

Located in the Square is the Ancestor Tree, sometimes known as the Eggun Tree. It's one of the largest in that area and perhaps one of the oldest trees in the city, dating back centuries. Over the years, it has become a popular stop for tour guides, who encourage visitors to put coins in the bark as "offerings" to the ancestors. This is a similar tradition to the "Wishing Trees" in England and Scotland. Authorities have urged tourists to stop this potentially damaging practice as coins release certain types of chemicals that can cause copper poisoning and kill the trees. Some voodoo practitioners, who consider the Square a spiritual base and still use it for rituals, are also against the practice. Sadly, this ties back to the complex historical dichotomy of the Square's history – trying to revere something while simultaneously damaging it. It's best to demonstrate your veneration for the Ancestor Tree with a photo.

Address 701 N. Rampart Street, New Orleans, LA 70116 | Hours Daily 8am–7pm | Tip Be sure and see the 12-foot statue of Louis Armstrong in his namesake park, created by Elizabeth Catlett.

19 Cool Zoo

Where the gators run

When most people see a giant alligator open its massive jaws, they scatter, but at the Cool Zoo splash park at Audubon Zoo, they stick around. Clearly modeled after "Spots," the white alligator at the Audubon Aquarium, this huge white alligator is a water slide that drops 400 gallons of water onto eager, excited kids (including grown-up kids) every 45 seconds. The 1.5-acre water park, located inside the zoo, also features a spider-monkey soaker, jumping water-spouts, water-spitting snakes, and custom-sculpted lion and elephant spin and spray big "sqwerts."

Gator Run, established in 2015, is a 750-foot lazy river that's three-feet deep and ten-feet wide. It takes approximately seven to ten minutes to make the full loop, either in an inner tube (provided) or just floating along. On the journey, you pass underneath four water cannons, two water curtains, jumping jets, and by two sand beaches. And if the animals are cooperative, you can catch glimpses of the elephants in the Asian Domain, the flock of flamingos near the South American boardwalk, and the aviary, all from the luxury of your tube.

For those under 48 inches, a life vest is required (and supplied), and for those over 21 years of age, there is also beer for sale at the concession stand, along with food, toys, towels, and swim diapers. There are lockers provided if you wish to stash your belongings and stroll around the zoo for a while.

The Cool Zoo is not a traditional mega water park but more of an intimate, friendly environment that caters mainly to children 12 and under; one of its three zones is exclusively for toddlers and younger children, although people of all ages can enjoy the sublimity of floating in the water and sipping a beverage of their choice. It may seem an odd coupling to have a water park inside a zoo, but whether you're an elephant or an 11-year-old, a grizzly or a grown-up, everyone loves to beat the heat with a little splish and splash.

Address Cool Zoo in Audubon Zoo, 6500 Magazine Street, New Orleans, LA 70118 | Hours Apr–Sept, Mon–Fri, 10am–5pm, Sat & Sun 10am–6pm (after Labor Day, weekends only) | Tip Monkey Hill in Audubon Zoo was constructed by the WPA in the 1930s. Legend says it was built to show New Orleans children what a hill looked like. It now features a five-level treehouse, wading pools, and a slide.

20 Cornstalk Fences

Iron cornfields with a past

New Orleans is not a place where images of cornstalks come to mind, but there are three intricate iron cornstalk fences attached to some of the city's most storied houses.

The most famous fence is at the historic Cornstalk Hotel in the French Quarter on Royal Street. The building was constructed as a private residence in 1816 for Francois Xavier Martin, Louisiana's first attorney general. The fence was built 40 years later. Each of the tree-trunk style fenceposts has a pumpkin at its base, and at the top are partially opened cornstalks that display the corn's yellow kernels. The hotel is said to be haunted, especially by an older woman who likes to walk up and down the hallway and peer out the window.

The next fence is in the Garden District on Fourth Street. The Italianate style 9,800-square-foot home was built for Colonel Robert Henry Short in 1859 by architect Henry Howard. During the Civil War, the house was seized by Federal Troops. It was used by the Federal Governor of Louisiana and later Major General Nathaniel P. Banks and his family. After the war, Short reclaimed his home. Although elaborate, this cornstalk fence is unpainted.

The other cornstalk fence in the Bayou St. John neighborhood on N. White Street is the most colorful. Known as the Dufour Plassan House after two of its previous owners – Cyprien Dufour, a former state senator, and Adolph Plassan, a cotton merchant – it was built in 1870 and is a mixture of French Colonial Plantation and Greek Revival style. The corn, morning glories, sunflowers, and pumpkins and the baskets of flowers atop some of the posts are all vividly painted.

All the fences were created by the ornamental ironworks manufacturer Wood, Miltenberger & Co. and are further linked by an identical rumor claiming that the gates were built because the owner's wife from Iowa missed seeing rows of corn. This rumor is about as likely as growing corn in a swamp, but it does give these beautiful buildings a touch of down-home hospitality.

Address 915 Royal Street, New Orleans, LA 70116; 1448 Fourth Street, New Orleans, LA 70130; 1206 N. White Street, New Orleans, LA 70119 | Tip The Andrew Jackson Hotel near the Cornstalk Hotel is reported to be haunted by five boys who died in a fire in 1794, when the hotel was used as a boarding school.

21 Country Club

Pool paradise

The Country Club has been an oasis in the heart of the Bywater for more than 45 years. This center-hall home blends finery, fantasy, and a bit of funk, and while it operates as a restaurant, bar, entertainment venue, and a pool, it creates one memorable experience.

The Country Club has three proper dining rooms and a lounge. All the framed art pieces throughout the space are by artist Louis St. Lewis. The murals are by artist Cindy Mathis, and create an equatorial vibe with whimsical elegance. The single parlor main dining room features Quaker parrots, a nod to the Argentina birds that mysteriously arrived in New Orleans in the 1960s and can be seen in the trees of the Uptown neighborhood. The double parlor dining room has flowers native to the city and to the tropics. In the lounge, known as the "butterfly room," vibrant butterflies adorn the walls.

The menu features a modern take on New Orleans classics, offering a wide array of small-plate dishes for those who want to try a bit of everything. Not to miss are their crab beignets and truffle mac-n-cheese. One of the pioneers in Drag Brunch, they offer two shows on Saturday and Sunday, and often sell out months in advance.

Continuing this paradise is the courtyard pool (entrance available by daily pass or yearly membership). The space is lush with foliage that transports you out of the city. The outdoor bar offers the same drink and food menu, over 100 lounge chairs dot the area, and there is a 20-person hot tub along with a separate seating area with tables. Outdoor and indoor showers and a dry sauna are available, and nothing is lost in the details. Ladies, check out the main indoor bathroom, which has a bubble wall and a mermaid. General manager Bert McComas states, however, that the best part of the Country Club is the wide mix of people it attracts. "People have made lifelong relationships here, which is the true beauty," McComas says. The tropical paradise is a bonus.

Address 634 Louisa Street, New Orleans, LA 70117 | Hours Daily 10am–11pm | Tip For another experience, Markey's Bar a few blocks up is an old-school watering hole that has been selling drinks for over 100 years.

22 Court of Two Sisters

A charmed gateway

The Court of Two Sisters restaurant was built around 1832, its name taken from a store owned by two sisters, Bertha and Emma Camors, from 1886 to 1906. It was then called the Shop of Two Sisters and sold fancy notions. The Camors were born to a mixed-race father and a white French mother. The sisters hid their racial identity, even taking on their mother's surname to further the subterfuge. The restaurant, which is known for its spacious courtyard, also has a air of mystique.

At its entrance are the Charm Gates, gifted by Queen Isabella II of Spain. It's reported that the gates are bewitched, and if you touch them, you'll be the recipient of good fortune. In the middle of the exposed-brick courtyard, there is an old well under a canopy of flowering vines. Originally called the Wishing Well – children would toss in coins to have their wishes granted – it became known as the Devil's Wishing Well as a nod to Marie Laveau, who was reputed to conduct some of her voodoo ceremonies there. Pirate Jean Lafitte is also alleged to have graced the courtyard when, as legend has it, he killed three men in one night, in three separate duels.

It's common for New Orleanians, with a whisper and wink, to claim ownership of anything supernatural, but there's at least one documented murder attached to the restaurant. In November 1952, Mrs. Amelia "Diddie" Cooper, a beautiful 29-year-old socialite, was found beaten and strangled to death in her uptown apartment. Her husband James Cooper, who had owned the Court of Two Sisters since the 1940s, was indicted for her murder. Cooper was found innocent in January 1954 despite overwhelming evidence. Two years later, Cooper dropped dead in his apartment above the restaurant from "strangulation" caused by an allergy. Most likely it was the high percentage of barbiturates in his blood, but there are whispers of karmic revenge from the grave

Today, the restaurant's magic comes primarily from its renowned jazz brunch, but it never hurts to give the Charm Gates a quick rub.

Address 613 Royal Street, New Orleans, LA 70130 | Hours Daily 9am–3pm, 5:30–9:30pm | Tip Next door is the Gallery Rinard, full of mirthful art by local artists.

23 Crescent City Farmers Market

Homegrown goodness

Market Umbrella is an independent nonprofit in New Orleans which has worked to improve New Orleans' economic and community health by providing the city with farmers markets. The Crescent City Farmers Market, which has been operating since 1995, offers three markets weekly, year-round, in different neighborhoods.

On Tuesday mornings, an Uptown parking lot across from the Mississippi River levee turns into a bustling market. On Thursday afternoons, the Lafitte Greenway in Mid City right next to Bayou St. John, becomes a hub of activity. On Sunday mornings, a section of City Park is transformed into an oak-lined marketplace. Children nibble on chocolate croissants, couples pick out fresh plants, and fishermen weigh freshly caught shrimp on small scales. Most shoppers know their favorite vendors by name, and families meet to shop together while their children (two-legged and four) play. Markets, according to Market Umbrella's Executive Director Angelina Harrison, are not just a place for commerce but an "accessible community space where people can gather," and provide "nutrition incentive and education programming," for the community.

Each of the markets offers fresh-grown items, which make up the majority of the markets' products. Fresh chicken, free-range eggs, pork, snapper, grouper, and even tenderized alligator meat are available. After the pandemic, more vendors started offering pre-prepared items such as fresh juices, avocado-cream frozen-fruit bars, nut butters, breakfast pastries, crawfish pies, kombucha, marinated feta, cheesecake, sourdough bread, tamales with homemade tortilla chips and salsas, and even bottles of rum. Gardeners also sell fresh-cut flowers, plants, and herbs. Many local restaurants stack their menus with items from the local vendors.

The market is a local trade hub that brings urban and rural together; hosting multiple events, activities, and tasting and cooking demonstrations, all while stressing the importance of shopping local.

Hours Tue 8am–noon in the parking lot at Uptown Square, 200 Broadway, New Orleans, LA 70118; Thu 3–6pm on the Lafitte Greenway, 500 N. Norman C. Francis Parkway, New Orleans, LA 70119; Sun 8am–noon in New Orleans City Park at the City Putt Parking Lot, 33 Dreyfous Drive, New Orleans, LA 70119 | Tip Café Reconcile is a nonprofit and restaurant in Central City that offers paid training in culinary arts for at-risk youth, allowing them to eventually enter the hospitality and restaurant industries of New Orleans. The menu includes such classics as blackened catfish, fried chicken, red beans and rice, and chicken, sausage, and okra gumbo.

24 Crescent Park

Following the rusty rainbow

Until 2014, the banks of the Mississippi River along the Marigny and Bywater neighborhoods were inaccessible from the active railroad tracks and large industrial buildings. The city transformed a no-man's land into a 1.4-mile, 20-acre, linear greenspace between the Public Belt Railroad tracks and the Mississippi River. It is now a beautiful vista filled with lush landscaping, benches, and picnic tables. It was named Crescent Park after the city's nickname, which derives from New Orleans' founder Jean-Baptiste Le Moyne, Sieur de Bienville, who first caught sight of the future New Orleans in the 17th century and wrote, "on the banks of the river is a place very favorable for the establishment of a post with one of the finest crescents on the river."

Unlike the Moonwalk – an approximately one-mile riverside promenade created in the 1970s across from Jackson Square, geared more toward tourists – Crescent Park has a much more local feel to it. Joggers, walkers, and roller skaters pass each other on the narrow smooth asphalt trail. Yoga practitioners sit in spots on the grass. Dog owners watch their pups frolic in the fenced-in dog run. All the while everyone enjoys the stunning views of the city and the Mississippi as a backdrop.

There are three entrances to the park. The first is at the convergence of Esplanade and Elysian Fields Avenues, and features a pedestrian bridge. The second, and beloved by locals, is at Piety Street, located at the midpoint of the park. The entrance has an arched steel bridge affectionately nicknamed the Rusty Rainbow. Designed by architect David Adjaye, it resembles a steampunk relic from a Terry Gilliam film with its unapologetic industrial form. It is the ideal spot to walk to the platform of the bridge and catch a bird's-eye view of the surroundings, but it is not ADA accessible. The third entrance is located at the southern end of the park on Bartholomew Street and is ADA compliant. The Piety and Bartholomew entrances have parking.

Address 2300 N. Peters Street; 3600 Chartres Street; 3900 Chartres Street | **Hours** Daily 6am–7pm | **Tip** Elizabeth's Restaurant, located near the Rusty Rainbow, is known for its signature praline bacon.

25 Crown & Anchor English Pub

TARDIS

If you want to know where Neil Timms, the owner of the Crown & Anchor English Pub, has lived, just check his arm. On his right arm are tattoos of the skylines of the cities where he has resided. Born in Coventry, England, as an IT specialist for InterContinental Hotels his job took him to London, Tashkent in Uzbekistan, Chicago, Atlanta, and New Orleans, where he decided to put down roots in 2004.

In 2010, his favorite local watering hole on Algiers Point, a place Timms calls "the greatest neighborhood in the city," went up for sale and he and his wife leapt at the opportunity.

The Crown & Anchor is the personification of an English pub. Vintage whiskey jugs hang from the low rafters, a pull-tab cigarette machine is tucked in the corner, dogs sit patiently by their owners, and the regulars clarify to the bartender, "No rush at all" when placing their drink order. The music is purposely low, according to Timms so people can have a "drink and conversation." It's almost a place where time stands still, so it's odd to find a spacecraft, a TARDIS (Time and Relative Dimension in Space).

Timms is a longtime fan of the BBC series *Doctor Who*, about a "Time Lord" who travels in a spacecraft called a TARDIS, which is disguised as a blue British police box. For his birthday in 2014, Timms' wife temporarily installed one as a surprise at the pub's entrance. Patrons loved it, so they made it permanent.

But a recent addition to the bar also gives the illusion of being transported into another realm – the sunny back patio. In 2024, the former parking lot was turned into an extension of the bar, which now features abundant outdoor seating and lawn games. A 200-inch screen and projector mainly show New Orleans Saints games, *Doctor Who* episodes, and the World Cup. But no matter where you are in time or space, at the Crown & Anchor you are always a local.

Address 200 Pelican Avenue, New Orleans, LA 70114 | Hours Sun–Thu 11am–midnight, Fri & Sat 11am–2am | Tip Finn McCool's Irish Pub in Mid City is considered the place to watch football leagues from around the world.

26 Dark Matters Oddities

Room of wonder

The historic Cucullu Row, just steps from Jackson Square, has the oldest intact row houses in the French Quarter. At one point, it housed the first celestial observatory constructed in the Americas, allowing people to glimpse the heavens. It was eventually reconstructed into the six three-story row houses that stand today.

It's a fitting location for Dark Matters Oddities & Artisan Collective, a store that personifies the past and reveres transformation. Artists (and husband and wife) Crystal Lea Nause and Joshua Gates were inspired by the concept of "wunderkammer," a German word which means "room of wonder" and represents a cabinet of curiosities. Wunderkammers were popularized in mid-16th-century Europe as repositories for objects that intersected science, art, and the astonishing. Nause designed the shop as a series of vignettes where cabinets and spaces hold everything from wet specimens of snakes, octopuses and frogs, religious relics, animal skulls, natural history specimens, secret society objects, medical implements, and vintage Halloween ephemera.

Over 40 artists, primarily local and from the Gulf Coast, exhibit their original art, including oil and acrylic paintings, bone art, embroidery, mixed-media assemblage dolls made from found objects that focus on anthropomorphic animals (such as a possum skull dressed in scrap fabric with real chicken feet), traditional taxidermy that follows natural history museum standards, and experimental taxidermy, such as myth-like jackalopes or animals that have alterations done to them.

Gates also has his own jewelry line called Uruz Metals, inspired by nature. Each piece is hand-fabricated with intention and works as a one-of-a-kind talisman.

Intention is key with Nause and Gates, who endeavor to curate unique found or created objects that spark wonder and curiosity. Their personal ethos is based on a quote from Ralph Waldo Emerson, and is apparent in every corner of the store: "There is no object so foul that intense light will not make beautiful… Even the corpse has its own beauty."

Address 822 Chartres Street, New Orleans, LA 70116 | Hours Mon, Wed & Thu noon–6pm, Fri–Sun 11am–7pm | Tip Disco Warehouse on Decatur Street has an artist market in their space, Thu–Sun (day markets noon–5pm; night markets 7pm–midnight).

27 Dat Dog's Chewbacchus Room

Bask in the glow of the sacred drunken Wookiee

The second floor at Dat Dog's Frenchmen Street location hosts the official shrine to the Intergalactic Krewe of Chewbacchus (IKOC): a twelve-foot-tall, six-armed, three-eyed icon, the "Sacred Drunken Wookiee." Chewbacchus, a portmanteau of Chewbacca from *Star Wars*, and Bacchus, the Roman god of wine, was founded in 2010 to (according to founder Ryan Ballard), "save the galaxy by bringing the magical revelry of Mardi Gras to the poor, disenfranchised, socially awkward, and generally weird masses" who might not have the opportunity to participate in a mainstream Mardi Gras parade. The sci-fi DIY parade has grown to over 150 sub-krewes, including the Death Star Steppers, Rolling Elliots, and Women of Wakanda. In 2014, IKOC became a religion, and for only $42 (everything costs $42 in Chewbacchus), you can become an ordained ChewbacchanALIEN Minister and officiate weddings, funerals, and other religious ceremonies.

Dat Dog, founded in 2011, is a New Orleans chain specializing in gourmet hot dogs and sausages. The menu includes sausages made from crawfish, alligator, duck, chicken, beef, as well as vegetarian options. Their 30-plus free toppings run the gamut from blackberry sauce to guacamole to étouffée, allowing customers to create their own "jazz improvisation in a bun."

The Golden Wookiee holds court behind the upstairs bar, looking out over the wall-to-wall Ewok Village, sci-fi reliquaries, and a half-dozen tables decorated by some of Chewbacchus' sub-krewes, including the Leijorettes (a mashup of Princess Leia and majorettes), Krewe of the Living Dead, and the Mystic Krewe of P.U.E.W.C. (People for the inclusion of Unicorns, Elves, and Whinebots in Chewbacchus). Patrons can enjoy the balcony and sip a Chewbacchus specialty cocktail like the Kalisti or Sith, and watch the hubbub of revelers below on the popular Frenchmen Street, or bask in the glow of the Drunken Wookiee.

Address Dat Dog, 601 Frenchmen Street, New Orleans, LA 70116 | Hours From 11am; upstairs bar from 6pm. Times vary for other locations at 3336 Magazine and 5030 Freret Street | Tip The 600 block of Frenchmen Street is crammed with musical venues where you can enjoy live music and a tasty cocktail: Café Negril (606), Apple Barrel (609), DBA (618), Spotted Cat (623), and Snug Harbor (626).

28 Deelightful Roux School of Cooking

Second to none

For Chef Dwynesha "Dee" Lavigne, there is no shame in being second. Lavigne, who had one grandmother who baked and one who cooked, loved from a young age how the smell of fresh bread could transform your mood and wanted to bring that feeling to others.

Lavigne earned a classical French culinary degree from the Culinary Institute of America. After working in the bakery department for Whole Foods in New Jersey for 15 years, she and her family moved back to New Orleans, where Lavigne started her own successful cupcake company, eventually becoming the Director of Culinary Programming for the Southern Food and Beverage Museum (SoFAB) and started a local televised cooking show. Then, the Smithsonian called about an exhibit on Lena Richards, a true trailblazer. Richards was the first African American woman in New Orleans to own her own cooking school, the first Black author to feature New Orleans Creole cuisine in her self-published cookbook, and the first African American, to host a cooking show, 14 years before Julia Child.

Inspired by Richards, Lavigne opened her own cooking school, at SoFAB – Deelightful Roux School of Cooking – and was stunned to discover that she was only the second African American woman in New Orleans to own her own cooking school. Dedicated to teaching others about Louisiana cuisine, Lavigne offers three public classes weekly that focus on Cajun and Creole cuisine. The classes are limited to 15 to keep the environment intimate and are 100 percent hands-on. Participants are taught step by step how to chop, sauté, and stir their dishes. Lavigne also teaches about the historical content of many of the ingredients and their importance to local cuisine. At the end, everyone gathers around the table to enjoy their creations and, according to Lavigne, enjoy the "beautiful experience of eating dinner, sharing stories, and talking with people you didn't know," making this experience second to none.

Address 1504 Oretha Castle, Haley Boulevard, New Orleans, LA 70113 | Hours Public classes available Mon, Thu & Fri 11am–1:30pm (lunch and curated guided tour of SoFAB included) | Tip The Southern Food and Beverage Museum is a nonprofit educational and cultural organization dedicated to the discovery and celebration of food, drink, and its related culture and folklife. It is also home to The Museum of the American Cocktail and the Culinary Heritage Sign Gallery.

29 Derby Pottery

Making history

An antique Victorian screen stands inconspicuously in the back corner of Derby Pottery. Purchased 25 years ago at a local antique store by ceramic artist Mark Derby, it is the cornerstone of the shop. Derby, a former ceramics professor at Tulane who tired of the academic life, created the business with his wife Ann Marie in 2000. Using primary sources, such as Victorian fireplace covers, ceiling tiles, and the screen in the store, the Derbys create molds and reimagine them into beautiful pieces that are artistic and often utilitarian. The result is a delicate blend of craft and fine art.

The front of the store is an assemblage of jewel-like glazed tiles: bats, fleur-de-lis, anchors, gryphons, hand-thrown bowls and pitchers, woodfired pieces, and large tile panels featuring cameos, Grecian women, or mermaids in cypress frames accentuated by small decorative tiles. But their art serves a larger purpose.

After Hurricane Katrina in 2005, many of the city's iconic street tiles were damaged. For Ann Marie it was a lightbulb moment. "I knew," she stated, "that this was our way to give back to New Orleans." The Derbys wanted them produced as they were in the late 1800s. The tiles are made with an encaustic inlay, which means the colors are not the product of a glaze but come from different colors and layers of clay, a process that takes about three days. In this method, the letters remain as the tile is worn down by the hundreds of feet stepping on them over time. The Derbys have produced tens of thousands of them for the city but also have them for sale to create customized keepsakes.

But Derby Pottery is not just a shop, it is also a studio. Everything is made on site and, depending on the day, you can witness the pieces being made. The furnishings in the store are also either salvaged from the street or purchased from former local shops. Part studio, part store, part homage to the community, every piece at Derby Pottery has a story that can be told for generations.

Address 2029 Magazine Street, New Orleans, LA 70130 | Hours Mon–Sat 11am–5pm | Tip In the time of horse and buggies, New Orleanians eschewed street signs for street tiles. You can find different brands over the decades, but you can recognize the Derbys' tiles by their signature gold border around the letter.

30 Dew Drop Inn

Swim, stay and sway

In 1939, Frank Painia opened a barbershop and bar. What started as a place to get a haircut and a drink became one of the most culturally significant businesses in New Orleans in the mid-20th century. Buying up adjacent businesses, Painia expanded the Dew Drop Inn into a nightclub, restaurant, and hotel. Operating during the time of the Jim Crow laws, the business was in the *Green Book,* a traveler's guide for African Americans that listed hotels, restaurants, service stations, and other establishments where they were legally allowed to be served.

The Dew Drop Inn was a magnet for upcoming jazz, blues, R&B, and rock and roll artists: Ray Charles, Irma Thomas, Allen Toussaint, Earl King, Sam Cooke, and James Brown all played at the inn. Little Richard once leapt up on stage and belted out a crude version of "Tutti Frutti" for the first time. The Dew Drop Inn offered comedy shows, snake charmers, ventriloquists, and female impersonators, including the legendary Patsy Vidalia, whom Painia hired as an emcee. Vidalia, who was openly gay, was a dazzling and charismatic performer whose Halloween Gay Ball was one of the largest parties of the year. Despite segregation laws, the Dew Drop Inn offered a haven where audiences and entertainers of different races mixed freely. Ironically, the Civil Rights Act of 1964 dealt a slow death blow to the inn. With the desegregation of public spaces, more venues opened.

The club closed around Painia's death in 1972, but the hotel remained open until Hurricane Katrina. Local developer Curtis Doucette later purchased it and lovingly restored it to a 400-person music venue, bar, swimming pool, and boutique hotel. The former 29 rooms are now 17 larger ones oozing with '50s-era nostalgia and themed after a notable person in the inn's history, including the James Booker, Little Richard and, of course, Patsy Vidalia rooms. Live Music Brunch on Saturdays plays songs from the Legends of the Dew Drop Inn. At the reopening in 2023, Irma Thomas returned, 63 years after her last appearance, ushering in a new era while honoring the past.

Address 2836 LaSalle Street, New Orleans, LA 70115, www.dewdropinnnola.com | **Hours** See website for opening hours and events | **Tip** The New Orleans Jazz Market, located in Central City, features a 370-seat theatre and plays host to performances by the New Orleans Jazz Orchestra and other renowned musicians.

31 Dive Bar Row

Far away from Bourbon Street

New Orleans is known for its iconic bars and drinking lifestyle. Louisiana was the last state to change its drinking age to 21. Initially, the state raised the drinking age in 1986 (de jure), but a loophole in the sales law allowed it to remain 18 (de facto) until 1995. The next year, the Louisiana Supreme Court ruled the law unconstitutional due to age discrimination but had to reverse it after facing threats of losing federal highway funding. This is also the state that has drive-thru daiquiris.

For years, locals gathered on Frenchmen Street for the experience of live music away from the tourists, but today many of them have migrated to St. Claude Avenue for cheap drinks and more off-beat acts. Siberia serves Latin Street Food and has shows like "Feys Gone Wild" with go-go dancing faeries and Elf Fortunetellers. The No Dice, formerly the Hi Ho Lounge, has a range of acts including witch doom bands, nu-metal, and glam rock. The AllWays Lounge & Cabaret has burlesque and drag shows with every possible theme, as well as queer storytelling and line dancing, movement classes, and sex trivia. Kajun's Karaoke proclaims itself "the best damn Karaoke Bar in NOLA" and hosts bingo on Tuesdays and Ladies' Night on Wednesdays, with women bartenders serving drink specials with liquor brands owned and made by women.

The undisputed ruler of the dive bars since the 1950s (and the furthest one away from Bourbon Street) is the Saturn Bar. The main room used to be a boxing ring, but decade-long regulars remember a time when it was piled high with air conditioners that the slightly eccentric owner O'Neil Broyard liked to tinker with but never appeared to fix. He would get irate if you asked for water or change. Today, it hosts a myriad of live performances, including burlesque, drag, and poetry readings – but not to miss is the Valparaiso Men's Chorus, which performs whenever the mood strikes and is made up of local musicians who perform sea shanties.

Address St. Claude Avenue: Siberia (2227); No Dice (2239); AllWays Lounge (2240); Kajun's Karaoke (2256); Saturn (3067) | **Hours** Vary, but all late night | **Tip** For a more traditional music venue on St. Claude Avenue, Sweet Lorraine's Jazz Club has been hosting traditional jazz for over 50 years.

32 Dooky Chase's Civil Rights Room

Small space, big legacy

Since its initial inception as a sandwich shop and lottery ticket outlet in 1939, Dooky Chase's Restaurant has been a place for cuisine and culture. In 1941, it transformed into a restaurant and barroom. Under the guidance of Leah Chase, who married Edgar Dooky Chase Jr. in 1946, it was turned into an upscale restaurant.

During segregation, it was one of the only fine-dining establishment in the United States that served African Americans. It was also the meeting place of civil rights leaders and volunteers. Anyone who was involved in the movement ate there when they were in New Orleans: Martin Luther King Jr., James Baldwin, Thurgood Marshall, and Ray Charles, among others. When interracial meetings were illegal, Dooky Chase's offered a safe space to gather and strategize.

On Twelfth Night 2025, and what would have been Leah Chase's 102nd birthday, the restaurant unveiled its new upstairs dining room, dedicated to the family's history in the Civil Rights Movement. Called the Legacy Room, the narrow stairs are almost emblematic of the movement's long and arduous journey, but each step has legislation on it that was passed either nationally or locally from discussions held in that very room. One of the murals, by local artist Ayo Scott, represents generations of the Chase family. Symbols are infused in the painting, including the barnyard rooster for Leah Chase, trumpet for Dooky Chase Jr., and the dove for their daughter Stella Chase. The other mural, created by Scott, Ron Bechet, and students from Xavier University, is of local leaders and captures a moment when – according to Tracie Haydel Griddin, granddaughter of Leah Chase and one of the restaurant operators, the Chase Family – employees and community members "worked lock and step for the Civil Rights Movement." The small mirror on the mural allows guests to see themselves sitting at the table with the individuals who created such change.

Address 2301 Orleans Avenue, New Orleans, LA 70119 | **Hours** Tue–Thu 11am–3pm, Fri 11am–3pm & 5:30–9pm, Sat 5:30–9pm; Legacy Room open to public when not booked for private events | **Tip** In front of the restaurant are what Dooky Chase calls Civil Rights Pavers, akin to the Hollywood Walk of Fame, but these markers include the names of local and national civil rights leaders who came to dine, and have discussions that were critical and essential to the movement.

33 Dr. Bob's Folk Art

Be nice and buy one

Whether you realized it or not, if you have spent any time in New Orleans, chances are that you've seen one of Dr. Bob's folk art pieces. His signature signs and paintings can be found in restaurants, clubs, and bars, especially his "Be Nice or Leave," sign, which has become a subculture mantra.

Located in what can only be described as a compound in the Bywater, Robert Shaffer, aka Dr. Bob, has been a fixture in the neighborhood since 1990. In the last few decades, the Bywater has witnessed the effects of gentrification. According to the New Orleans Date Center, since 2000 the neighborhood has gone from 61 percent Black and 32 percent White to 17 percent Black and 72 percent White. Residents have seen many family-owned restaurants and corner stores that have stood for generations make way for upscale fusion restaurants and high-end specialty stores that seem to open up and close down on a rotating basis. Through all of this, Dr. Bob has remained.

The parking lot is worth a visit alone. Large sculptures made from various recycled wares that are fashioned into mythical creatures (or roosters), and skeletons made entirely from bottle caps, mix with the occasional Santa Claus statue, broken-down cars, and piles of debris. It's difficult to differentiate between trash and treasure, but to Dr. Bob, it's all treasure. His gallery is akin to a large warehouse shed, and it is packed with his funky folk art of local wildlife (he often uses alligator teeth for some of his pieces), caricatures of local characters and musicians, and a sort of mystic swamp mojo palmistry. Almost all of Dr. Bob's pieces incorporate objects that he has found on the street or dumpster or have been donated to him. He has also added to his repertoire with "Be Gay and Stay," "Shut Up and Eat," and "Shalom, Y'all."

His unique folk art style has landed his pieces in the Smithsonian Institute, the Center for Southern Folklore in Memphis, and the New Orleans House of Blues, but the affordable prices on most of his pieces make it possible for anyone to own a piece of his creativity.

Address 3027 Chartres Street, New Orleans, LA 70117 | Hours Daily 10am–3pm but don't be surprised if it is closed, based on Dr. Bob's whim | Tip The Green Project is a nonprofit salvage store where you can purchase everything from light fixtures to sinks and antique side tables.

34 Evacuspots

Friendly warnings

Situated around the city are tall, austere metal stick figures appearing to be waving to a friend across the way or hailing a cab. These are not simply feel-good sculptures but are markers designating the "Evacuspots" people will gather at if they need help in getting out of the city in the event of a mandatory evacuation.

Created in the wake of Hurricane Katrina, these 12-foot sculptures were commissioned by the New Orleans Arts Council and Evacuteer.org, a post-Katrina philanthropic organization founded to help support the New Orleans Office of Homeland Security and Emergency Preparedness as part of the City Assisted Evacuation Plan.

Over 80 artists from all over the country submitted proposals. The key to the design was that it had to effectively signal a safe meeting point in case of an emergency but not be a constant reminder of possible imminent disaster, meaning it had to be cheerful enough to be viewed every day but clear that its purpose was to gather people in case of a meteorological catastrophe.

The winning design was created by Boston artist Douglas Kornfield. It didn't hurt Kornfield that his design was also evocative of someone raising their hands to catch some Mardi Gras beads, something New Orleanians could relate to. Kornfield believes that the reason he won the competition was "because it's quintessentially New Orleans, but it's also universal to everybody," he told the *Times-Picayune.*

The lofty silver men are sandblasted to create a satiny sheen, made to resist rust, are anchored with concrete pads to prevent toppling, and are expected to last for 100 years. The leg of each sculpture is marked with a plaque that has the rules of evacuation: one small bag, no alcohol or weapons, and pets must have IDs and be leashed or in carriers.

The sculptures might represent a method to get out of the city, but they have become a part of the city in the truest sense.

Address Located in various areas around New Orleans | Tip Check out New Orleans' electoral utility boxes at stoplights across town. The boxes were part of a project started by Jeannie Tidy in 2010 to beautify the neighborhoods by having local artists paint various NOLA-related images on them.

35 Fats Domino Home

A symbol of roots and recovery

In the Lower Ninth Ward stands a house that is an emblem to remembering your roots – Fats Domino's home. Born in 1928 to a French Creole family in New Orleans, Domino learned the piano from his cousin, eventually signing with Imperial Records in 1949. His first single "The Fat Man," (which references Rampart and Canal Streets) is cited by musical historians as the first rock and roll single. He followed with singles such as "Ain't That a Shame," "Blueberry Hill," "Walking to New Orleans," "Blue Monday," and "I'm Walking." Domino would eventually sell over 65 million records, making him the second top-selling rock and roll artist during the early days, just behind Elvis Presley. His piano-playing was remarkable at the time for its lack of excessive exuberance. Artists like Jerry Lee Lewis and Little Richard were known for their flamboyant stage presence, jumping up, kicking back the stool, or dancing next to the piano, but Domino had the exact opposite approach. Even for the most frenetic song, Domino always played with a tranquil, relaxed manner.

This translated to his personal life. Domino was known for his modesty and homebody tendencies. With his success, Domino could have lived anywhere but he chose the neighborhood he grew up in, hosting dignitaries and famous musicians with the same casual ease he did with his friends and family. His popularity waned during the mid-1960s, but he continued touring for another 30 years and regularly performed at the New Orleans Jazz and Heritage Festival.

During Hurricane Katrina, Fats Domino was reported missing. For three days, people around the world worried until word of his dramatic rescue by boat from the second story of his flooded home surfaced. Domino returned to the stage for his final Jazz Fest appearance in 2006. Under the direction of the Louisiana State Museum, Domino's house and his white Steinway piano were restored, but he spent his last few years living on the West Bank. Domino's home in the Lower Ninth Ward remains as a tribute to his legacy.

Address 1208 Caffin Avenue, New Orleans, LA 70117 | Tip For hardcore music lovers, Cosimo Matassa's J&M Recording Studio – where greats such as Fats Domino, Little Richard, Danny Barker, Jerry Lee Lewis, Ray Charles and Professor Longhair recorded – is located at 838–840 N. Rampart Street. It is now a laundromat but was designated a historic landmark in 1999.

36 Fifi Mahony's

Wig paradise

Do you need an old-fashioned silver sailboat attached to a Marie Antoinette-style wig? Maybe a plastic surfer riding a wave of hair atop a vividly blue wig with hibiscus flowers planted at the bottom, ready to catch his fall, a green wig softly teased out with peacock feathers and jewels that look like a natural element to your coif, or a long blonde bouffant decorated in pink flowers and feathers that looks like Dolly Parton and Marie Antoinette had a child? Fifi Mahony's has it all and more.

Since 1997, Fifi's has been *the* place to shop for wigs, cosmetics, and anything sparkly. Although Fifi's specializes in custom wigs, they also have rows upon rows of wigs such as tangerine beehives, rainbow-colored afros, and scarlet pageboy bobs, with a selection of colors and styles so diverse and appealing that it is like an ice cream shop for your head. One scoop or two? With more than 100 wigs to choose from, starting around $45, customers can either shop and go, or with a stylist for customization, and purchase accessories for extra adornment.

But if you're looking for something a little more permanent, in 2013 Fifi's opened its own salon inside the store that offers cuts, colors, extensions, brows, and makeup services. Owner Marcy Hesseling says that on many occasions clients will love their wig color so much that they get their hair dyed to match the same day. But even with its kitschy opulence, Fifi's also carries traditional wigs, catering to clients suffering from hair loss and anyone opting to blend in instead of standing out. Glitter, cosmetics (Ben Nye as well as their own custom line), flash eyelashes, miniature-sequined top hats, and fascinators with a glut of feathers, can all be found at Fifi's underneath a lavish crystal chandelier with a plaster medallion of nymphs looking down as you shop. And if you need to validate your shopping excursion? You can simply state that you were curious to see the former home of General P. G. T. Beauregard and his son René, who lived here from 1868 to 1875.

Address 934 Royal Street, New Orleans, LA 70116 | Hours Mon–Sat 11am–7pm, Sun noon–6pm | Tip If looking at all those candy-colored wigs triggers your sweet tooth, dessert shop Sucré is located at 636 Royal Street and carries multi-colored macaroons, chocolates, gelato, and pastries.

37 Flooded Museum

Outside looking in

A modest brown brick house in the Gentilly neighborhood stands as a reminder of the horrific devastation of Hurricane Katrina in August 2005. Only visible through the front windows is a life-sized diorama that reconstructs the interior of a flooded home. Moldy furniture, a toppled-over piano, overturned table, children's toys scattered on the floor, and wallpaper, peeling and stained, hanging listlessly from the wall. All of this is framed with an ominous water mark around the walls. This voyeuristic approach evokes the emotions of a family returning home to find everything they owned destroyed.

Next door is a 100-foot covered walkway featuring six museum-quality exhibit panels that tell the story through text and multiple photographs of the levee breaches during Hurricane Katrina. At the center is a large rectangular green space with native plants, a walkway, and trees. Brightly colored chairs are scattered about for visitors to relax and take in the scope of the project. Facing the levees is a 16-foot by 8-foot steel and cast aluminum sculpture from Carl Joe Williams and Young Artist Movement (YAM) entitled *Unity*. On pieces of the painted aluminum are words such as "heal," "pride," and "strength."

The project was the brainchild of Levees.org. The organization purchased a gutted house next to the London Avenue Canal and obtained a permit to build the exhibit in partnership with the neighborhood residents. Sandy Rosenthal, the founder of the organization, worked with various independent experts to present an accurate step-by-step portrayal on how the improperly built levees led to the catastrophic effects of Hurricane Katrina. Many families, who had deep generational roots in the neighborhood, had their entire homes picked up and moved across the street due to the strength of the flood waters. This area, which once symbolized death and destruction to so many, now stands for rebirth and resilience.

Address 5000 Warrington Drive, New Orleans, LA 70122 | Hours Viewable 24 hours | Tip The Hurricane Katrina Memorial on Canal Boulevard is located on the site of the former Charity Hospital Cemetery where the unclaimed were buried, as were those who donated their bodies to science.

38 Flying Horses Carousel

A ride through time

On a carousel in City Park, the horses fly. For almost 125 years, children and adults have climbed aboard the ride and been taken on a fantastical journey on the last antique wooden carousel in Louisiana, and one of only about 100 in the country. Housed in a decagon, a 10-sided Victorian-inspired pavilion, the carousel, still operating with its original motor, was placed on the National Register of Historic Places in 1986.

The carousel has 56 hand-carved wooden animals. Fifty-three of them are horses in various states of movement including "prancers," which keep their two hind legs on the ground; "standers," which have three feet on the ground, and "jumpers," which have all four feet in the air. But what gives the attraction its nickname – the "Flying Horses Carousel" – is the 30 "flyers," the horses that move up and down.

The horses are all unique and range in different colors from chestnut to dapple-gray to gold, with real horsehair for their tails. The saddles and bridles are painted in a gamut of colors, from delicate pastels to brilliant hues of rich purple and red, and many are adorned with faux jewels. Adding to their distinctiveness are their varying head positions and expressions, including some with curled lips and lolling tongues. Also joining this menagerie are Leo, a 500-pound lion with a dark saddle with gold chain links, Cammie the Camel with a fringed blanket, and Geoffrey the Giraffe, whose blanket appears to have gold tassels and bells. There are also two chariots for those who prefer to sit side by side and admire the vibrant wildlife instead of riding it. The alligator is for display only and has a saddle with magnolia blossoms, an egret, crawfish, and Krewe of Rex doubloon. And just as real horses have groomers, these are maintained by WRF Designs, a father-and-son team who regularly restore the wear and tear that comes with time and many enthusiastic riders.

Address 1 Victory Drive, New Orleans, LA 70124 | Hours Mar–Nov Sat & Sun 11am–6pm | Tip The Carousel Garden Amusement Park in City Park has 18 rides including Bumper Cars, the Ferris Wheel, and the Live Oak Ladybug Roller Coaster.

39 French Quarter Alleys

Quick trips through time

While the French Quarter is famous for many of its streets, particularly raucous Bourbon Street and the elegant shops on Royal Street, lesser known are some of its pedestrian alleys.

Pirate's Alley, located between St. Louis Cathedral and The Cabildo (originally the seat of Spanish colonial city hall and now a museum) is the subject of local lore as a place where pirates gathered. On this one-block cobblestone pedestrian walkway is Faulkner House Books, a bookstore located at the former house of William Faulkner, and Pirates Alley Café & Olde Absinthe House, a narrow bar with pirate and nautical themes rumored to be the closest bar in the country to a church, hence the *Quiet: Church Zone* sign.

Intersected by Pirate's Alley is Cabildo Alley, another cobblestone walkway, which connects to St. Peter Street and is the width of The Cabildo building.

On the northeast side of the cathedral between the Presbytère (the former residence of the Capuchin monks and now a state museum) is Pere Antoine Alley, named after a Capuchin friar who was controversial in his time for shepherding to everyone, including the enslaved, poor, and prisoners. He was so beloved that when he was suspended in 1805 for a dispute with the vicar-general, the citizens elected Antoine their parish priest, a post he kept until his death in 1829 at 81 years old. It's a fitting tribute to have the alleys flanking the cathedral named after both pirates and a priest.

Located by the French Market, the country's oldest public market, is Dutch Alley, named after New Orleans' first African American mayor Ernest "Dutch" Morial (1929–1989). This two-block cobblestone alley is brimming with historic buildings and food stands. Its jewel is the Dutch Alley Artist Co-Op, which showcases works from more than 25 local artists. It gives visitors a chance to meet and speak with many of the painters, printmakers, ceramicists, photographers, and jewelry makers, and to purchase one-of-a-kind items.

Address Pirate's Alley between St. Louis Cathedral and The Cabildo; Cabildo Alley intersected between Pirate's Alley and ending at St. Peter Street; Pere Antione Alley between St. Louis Cathedral and the Presbytère; Dutch Alley behind the intersection of Decatur and St. Peter Streets, between St. Philip and Dumaine Streets | Tip Meat lovers like to take their picture with Jacques the Butcher outside Dutch Alley Artist Co-Op. This life-sized bronze statue of an old-time butcher, wearing a bowler hat and bow tie, has a cleaver in one hand and a T-bone steak in the other.

40 Friday Night Fights

Boxing with a twist

Over time, New Orleans' impact on the sport of boxing has been largely forgotten. The Irish pugilists ignited interest in the sport in the 1830s, and over the decades, it evolved from makeshift rings in rural areas and barges anchored out on the Mississippi River to evade the law to serving as the site of the first ever heavyweight prize fight in 1870. The 1892 heavyweight title fight between John L. Sullivan and Jim Corbett at the Olympic Club in the Bywater is considered by sports historians as the beginning of the modern boxing era. The 1978 fight between Muhammad Ali and Leon Spinks, and the "No Más" fight between Sugar Ray Leonard and Roberto Durán in 1980, both taking place in the Superdome, cemented New Orleans' reputation as the epicenter of boxing. Boxing's popularity waned in the 1980s, but a new blend of performance and pugilism has emerged in New Orleans.

Entering into the ring: Mike Tata, a former Marine and New Yorker. Tata is a boxing enthusiast who claims he enjoys instigating a fight more than being in one. After seeing the rising costs of gym ownership in New York, Tata moved to New Orleans and opened his gym in 2005; it flooded eight months later during Hurricane Katrina. He reopened his gym in a new location and shortly after started Friday Night Fights, a frenetic fete of fancy footwork featuring boxers and varied entertainment. Aside from the 10 to 12 amateur bouts offered, Tata has dance krewes, burlesque dancers, hot-dog eating contests, drag queens, beer-chugging contests, circus performers, rappers, and twerking teams – all to keep the momentum and the crowd engaged and involved.

The fights are offered quarterly. Each event features eight fights (male and female) of three rounds each. You might see a Jesuit priest take on a college student to two rising lightweights battling it out. Look for the fancy footwork from the crowd and the combatants as the entertainment moves as quickly as a knock-out punch.

Address 1632 Oretha Castle Haley Boulevard, New Orleans, LA 70113 | **Hours** Gym daily 9am–8pm; fights take place quarterly | **Tip** Oretha Castle Haley Boulevard has experienced a resurgence in recent years with restaurants, museums, and music, including the New Orleans Jazz Market, Casa Borrega, Southern Food & Beverage Museum, and the Ashe Cultural Arts Center.

41 Garden Totem Poles

Whimsy on the bayou

All along the streets and banks of the Bayou St. John neighborhood are vibrant ceramic pieces adorning signposts and poles. These are the work of potter Peggy Bishop. When Bishop first started working with clay in 2000, she decided to beautify her neighborhood by placing cylinders on top of the *No Parking* signs along the bayou. Soon Bishop discovered that she liked to make bigger things and transitioned into creating yard art. Bishop started covering the nearby signposts completely with brightly colored local wildlife, domestic pets, planets, voodoo dolls, abstract shapes, and even aliens. Calling them Garden Totem Poles, each of the pieces are made by hand, thrown on the wheel, and then altered.

The pieces can be found all over the Bayou neighborhood, particularly Ursuline Avenue. One of these poles is decorated in brightly colored beads, another has some cylinders with motifs representing the city, and a three-dimensional sculpture of a dog's head sticks out its tongue on a third. The most recent one is in the small triangle-shaped park Kennedy Place in monochromatic blues with vines at the base that weave into an octopus stretching up to a majestic pelican.

Bishop has made about 10 of the public sculptures for the city. She often starts with a general theme for each piece, but admits she has been known to "throw together" whatever she has in her studio. The sculptures are designed to be placed on three-quarter inch steel poles. No two pieces are alike, and they average five to six feet in height. Many of the pieces are found prominently placed in private front yards and gardens, but if someone commissions Bishop to make one for a public space, she gives them a discount. "I hope they bring a kind of joy to people," Bishop says of her whimsical statues, "perhaps a smile." They do, placing her art on a pedestal to epitomize grassroot public art, much like the pedestals on her very own Garden Totem Poles.

Address Along Moss Street on Bayou St. John and throughout the Bayou St. John neighborhood | Tip Pal's Lounge is the ultimate neighborhood dive bar and a favorite of British actress Helen Mirren, who often visits it when she is in town. She even has a drink named after her, the "Helen F#@*in Mirren."

42 General Laundry

Mayan masterpiece

With all of New Orleans' distinct architecture, the General Laundry stands out for its unique Mayan and Aztec Revival style. The nearly block-long building in the Treme is embellished with burgundy, green, yellow, and blue geometrical patterns, lush tropical depictions, and sunflower and sunrise motifs.

A fire in February 1929 destroyed the laundry. Refusing to quit, President Robert Chapoit had the building rebuilt in record time, and in May 1930, held a grand reopening where over 5,000 individuals came out to marvel at the most modern laundry plant in the South.

Chapoit, a marketing master, invited church, civic, and political organizations to hold their meetings in the reception room. Bridge parties convened there with no charge while porters served tea. "Style Shows" were held, where striking women and "Adonis-like" men modeled the latest fashions. Chapoit's most brilliant ploy, however, was hosting monthly "Visitors' Hours." Hundreds would flock for a tour of the plant in full operation while enjoying drinks, hors d'oeuvres, and luxurious attendance prizes. Other laundry plants in the States and Canada later mimicked the popular event. Chapoit claimed that he wanted to let housewives spend more time with their family. One ad publicized that there would be "HELLZAPOPPIN" if Dad's shirts were badly laundered, and it was best to let General Laundry do the job.

The advent of the home washing machine was the business' death knell, and Chapoit sold it in 1945. Since then, the building has been a diaper service, U.S. Postal Service, scrap metal collection, and now a recycling company. It was added to the National Register of Historic Places in 1974, and over the decades, the building has escaped the wrecking ball multiple times. Abandonment, vandalism, and the climate have led to its deterioration. One of the few remaining Art Deco buildings is now littered with broken windows, graffiti on its stucco walls, and foliage growing through some of the roof gaps. What was once born from the ashes now awaits a rebirth born from neglect.

Address 2544 St Peter Street, New Orleans, LA 70119 | Hours Viewable from the outside only | Tip The Municipal Auditorium located in Louis Armstrong Park, a five-story, Italian Renaissance-style building, was completed in 1930. Once a touchstone for the city's musical heritage, it has been abandoned since Hurricane Katrina as city leaders fight over its future.

43 Germaine Wells Mardi Gras Museum

Fit for a queen

For three decades, Germaine Cazenave Wells operated Arnaud's, a landmark French Quarter restaurant. But for almost her entire life, she ruled the city's social scene. Born in 1902, Wells was the daughter of French immigrant Leon Bertrand Arnaud Cazenave, who opened Arnaud's in 1918. His elaborate lifestyle and regal manners earned him the nickname "Count." Wells, a singer and actress, inherited his noble demeanor and love of grandeur. Wells sang and acted in various stage productions. Her father was appalled at the idea of Wells performing for money, which prompted her to quip that he didn't give his food away for free. But Wells didn't just preside over the stage, she reigned as Queen of 22 Mardi Gras balls from 1937 to 1968, a record. Since it would be considered in bad taste to wear the same ballgown twice, Wells had an original gown made for each ball.

When the Count died in 1948, Wells took over the restaurant, despite not even being able to cook. Famous for its French Creole cuisine, the restaurant has a main dining room and multiple private dining rooms. In 1957, Wells was named one of the country's top hostesses. The following year, she displayed some of her gowns on mannequins.

In 1956, Wells started the Easter Parade. Participants dressed in fancy attire with the ladies in elaborate bonnets riding in mule-drawn carriages, starting at her mansion on 544 Esplanade Avenue and ending at St. Louis Cathedral for mass.

In 1983, the make-believe monarch officially opened the Germaine Cazenave Wells Mardi Gras Museum. It included outfits worn by her mother (the oldest from 1941), her father, and daughter, whom she named Arnaud and who died in 1977. It also has Carnival masks, tiaras, elaborate krewe invitations, and party favors. Wells died in 1977 and was buried in Metairie Cemetery. Ever the Queen, she was buried in a gold lamé gown.

Address Located in Arnaud's, 813 Bienville Street, New Orleans, LA 70112 | Hours Mon–Sat 5:30–9pm, Sun 10am–1:30pm | Tip Germaine Wells' Easter Parade continues today. Now it is called the Historic French Quarter Easter Parade and has ladies in Easter bonnets riding in carriages and convertibles. It starts, however, at Antoine's Restaurant.

44_Gondola Rides in City Park

A taste of Venice

Robert Dula remembers the exact moment he wanted to be a gondolier. The 17-year-old was in his hometown of Lafayette, Louisiana when he saw Roger Moore as James Bond in the movie *Moonraker*, zipping through Venice in a "souped-up, high-performance gondola." Dula's dream faded, but in the early 2000s it was reignited, and he went to Boston to train as a gondolier. In 2003, he travelled to Venice for the first time to purchase his own handcrafted gondola, christened *Bella Mae* (after his mother).

Dula's gondola career started in Pensacola, Florida in 2004, but five months later, Hurricane Ivan hit. Dula lost his home and business but saved his gondola by sinking it in 10 feet of water. He recovered *Bella Mae* and came to New Orleans in March of 2005, only to have Hurricane Katrina hit in August. Dula sank his gondola again, this time in the lagoon behind the Sculpture Garden. *Bella Mae* remained there for over a month before Dula was able to return and rescue her. He returned to operations in 2010.

Dula, who is Cajun and admits to being "not a bit Italian," is the only gondolier on the Gulf Coast. "It's like floating on air," Dula says of the ride. *Bella Mae* can seat up to six adults (dogs ride for free), and the leisurely trip around City Park takes about an hour, traveling under multiple bridges, gliding past egrets, turtles, and herons while you view large art sculptures, majestic live oaks, and various historical structure in the park. It is B.Y.O.B., so travelers can bring their own wine or champagne, and Dula provides the ice and the music – everything from Andrea Bocelli to Aaron Neville to Louis Armstrong. To date, Dula has witnessed almost 1,000 marriage proposals. And for those nervous about popping the question? Dula assures that all of them have said yes on the *Bella Mae.* During the middle of one memorable proposal, a seagull actually pooped on the man! The woman still said yes. Surely 007 would approve.

Address Big Lake Trail in City Park, New Orleans, LA, 70124, www.nolagondola.com | **Hours** Hours vary – check website; advance booking required | **Tip** Located next to Nola Gondola is Wheel Fun Rentals. You can rent a swan boat, kayak, or canoe by the hour and paddle about the Big Lake; or hire a surrey or wide collection of bicycles to explore City Park even more. Fun fact: the track was designed for the 1992 Olympic trials!

45 Greetings from NOLA

Your own selfie postcard

Located in the Irish Channel is a giant vintage postcard-style mural: "Greetings from NOLA." It is from artists (and couple) Lisa Beggs and Victor Ving. In 2015, the couple, who had painted a "Greetings from Chinatown" mural the previous year, packed up their RV and left to travel around the country with a mission to paint a mural in every state. To date, they have painted over 70 murals in 30 states. These murals, unique to each place, have become a bucket-list item for many travelers.

The murals are based on Beggs' photographs of nearby landmarks, iconic sites, cultural references, and national parks. Ving uses these images as inspiration for painting the murals. More importantly, the couple take suggestions from locals. They arrived in New Orleans during Mardi Gras 2019 to create this mural. With help from local business owners of La Belle Nouvelle Orleans and the Renaissance Shop, who helped them find their location on Magazine and Josephine Streets, they even crowdsourced some of the funding from other local businesses to help cover the cost of supplies. Local retailer Mystic Blue Signs contributed their lettering design for the "Greetings From" in the yellow box.

The 12-foot by 18-foot mural took five days to complete, a little bit longer than usual as they sometimes took breaks from their work to walk down to St. Charles Avenue to catch a parade.

Beggs and Ving incorporated local images into the mural, such as Mardi Gras masks, St. Louis Cathedral, the Superdome, a streetcar, and a fleur-de-lis. The pelican and the crawfish came from direct suggestions from locals. Ving, who has traveled all over the world, stated that sometimes cities can feel repetitive, but he loved the international feel to New Orleans with its architecture, food, art, and "grittiness." Of course, what he found most "refreshing" was the South's legendary hospitality. And when he missed his old delis in New York City, Stein's Market & Deli made him feel like he was back in Manhattan.

Address 2014 Magazine Street, New Orleans, LA 70130 | Tip Stein's Market & Deli on Magazine Street is a Jewish and Italian deli serving traditional and specialty sandwiches using top-quality meat, breads, and cheeses.

46 Guardian's Wall

A monument to AIDS victims

Since the start of the HIV/AIDS epidemic, over 40 million people have lost their lives to AIDS-related illness across the globe. Located outside the effervescent French Quarter is a sculpture to commemorate the victims and families affected by AIDS.

In the late 1990s, an international competition was launched to create an outdoor monument in New Orleans for those affected by the disease. Artist Tim Tate was in a French Quarter bar when he met a couple heading up the fundraising initiative for the project. When they discovered he was a sculptor, they asked if he had anything appropriate, and Tate drew out a sketch on a napkin. Called "Guardian's Wall," the napkin wasn't included in his official application, but was inspired by his impromptu sketch.

Tate worked with local glass artist Mitchell Gaudet to complete the project, an 8-foot-high by 35-foot-wide curved steel structure with 34 translucent glass multicultural faces of men and women cast from locals who were affected by the epidemic, in concentric bronze circles.

Located in Washington Square Park in the Marigny, which has one of the highest LGBTQ+ populations in the city, the emotive sculpture simultaneously captures both loss and hope. It is surrounded by a fan-like pattern of engraved granite stones with the names of those who died from AIDS-related illnesses on it, and a plaque listing the supporters of the project that includes a quote from Mexican author Laura Esquivel at the bottom: "When do the dead die? When they are forgotten."

Each year on December 1, World AIDS Day, the Office of Health Policy and AIDS Funding (OHP) has a wreath-laying ceremony in front of the memorial to recognize and pay respects to those who are living with HIV and those we have lost to the epidemic. "I hope that when people enter that space, that it feels restful and contemplative," Tate says. "The sculpture has much gravitas, so I hope everyone slows down for just a minute to remember those lost."

Address Washington Square Park, 700 Elysian Fields, New Orleans, LA 70116 | Tip The Queen's Head Pub, located upstairs on the wrap-around balcony at Good Friends Bar, a local gay bar, has a Victorian vibe with none of the social hang-ups.

47 H. Rault Locksmith

The secret key

Magazine Street is known for its multi-generational, family-owned restaurants and local shops of antiques, vintage clothing, and specialty items. But only one can claim the honor of being the oldest operating business on Magazine Street – H. Rault Locksmith.

French immigrant Joseph Rault first opened a gunsmith shop on Bourbon Street in 1845. His son, Henri, learned locksmithing and they moved the business to Magazine Street, bouncing around to a few different locations on the street until they settled at 3027 Magazine Street in 1947. They have remained here ever since.

The shop, which was restored in the 1990s, has evolved over the years, but at its heart it is still a locksmith store, the second oldest in the country. Locals come from all over the city to get their modern (and vintage) locks and keys repaired, replaced, and installed. It is the place to go in New Orleans for 19th-century doorknobs, door handles, furniture locks, shutter hardware, and keyholes. It also has one of the largest collections of key blank skeletons in the country. Additionally, H. Rault has a broad selection of modern fixtures. But over the last few decades, the store has evolved. It is now also part museum, part store where customers can view vintage pieces such as antique skeleton keys, door knockers, tools, mid-20th-century metal signs, and brass cash registers, as well as learning about the history of the store and locksmithing. It also sells one-of-a-kind handmade jewelry created with original antique hardware. As it states in various signs all over the store, these original pieces of jewelry are available in store only or, as they write, they are only available "where you are standing." They do not take special requests or alter the jewelry in any way. You get what you get. But there is plenty to choose from as the pieces vary from necklaces and lavaliers made from vintage locks and keys to bracelets created from brass strike plates. And from wherever you are standing in the store, it's always a good deal.

Address 3027 Magazine Street, New Orleans, LA 70115 | Hours Mon–Fri 9am–5pm, Sat noon–4pm | Tip There are plenty of other vintage stores on Magazine Street, including Magazine Antique Mall (3017), The OW Home (2805), and Vagabond Vintage Clothing (3033).

48 Hot Tin

Cocktails with a view

Located on the historic St. Charles Avenue is the Pontchartrain Hotel. Named after Louis XIV court's Count de Pontchartrain (as is our Lake Pontchartrain), the hotel was originally a high-end 14-story apartment building that opened in 1927. In the 1940s, it was transformed into a chic hotel that housed such notable guests as Frank Sinatra, Rita Hayworth, and Jim Morrison.

In 2016, the hotel underwent a major renovation, keeping its tropically exotic old-school theme but updating its 106 rooms with 21st-century amenities. The renovation also included a panoramic rooftop and three more epicurean destinations, including the Jack Rose, a ground-level restaurant serving Italian, French and Spanish dishes where one room has a portrait of Lil Wayne surrounded by multiple antique-style paintings of still life flowers; the Silver Whistle Café, a breakfast café and coffee shop reminiscent of a French café, that overlooks St. Charles Avenue; and the Bayou Bar, a funky bar swathed in warm earth colors that has a small elevated pub menu and features live music Tuesdays through Saturdays.

The jewel in the crown is the Hot Tin rooftop bar offering a 270-degree view of Downtown New Orleans and the Mississippi River. Formerly a penthouse, the reimagined space was modeled after a 1940s artist's loft with a luxurious promiscuity and a magpie of assorted curios and tchotchkes that all blend together to create a relaxed but indulgent experience. Hot Tin serves strictly beer, wine, and craft cocktails. Two notable beverages include the Rita Hayworth, made with tequila, chipotle chilis, apricots, and lime, and the High Violet, composed of vodka, Lillet Blanc, crème de violette, lime, plum, bitters, and soda.

The view, however, is the pièce de résistance. An elevated experience (both literally and figuratively), one can view beautiful sunsets over the city's entire skyline, from the Superdome to the Mississippi River bridge, on the spacious balcony.

Address The top floor of the Pontchartrain Hotel, 2031 St. Charles Avenue, New Orleans, LA 70130 | Hours Sun–Thu 2pm–midnight, Fri & Sat 2pm–2am | Tip Because of the gorgeous view, the drinks can be a bit pricey at the Hot Tin. The Avenue Pub down the street is more affordable, and has over 40 beers on tap, a full menu, and a wide assortment of whiskeys.

49 Ignatius J. Reilly Statue

Watching for signs of bad taste

In front of New Orleans' Hyatt Centric Hotel stands a statue of a slightly disheveled-looking man. It pays homage to one of the great New Orleans literary characters: Ignatius J. Reilly, an educated, flatulent, and slothful 30-year-old narcissist who lives with his patient, but perpetually flustered and overweening, mother Irene.

Set in the early 1960s, John Kennedy Toole's novel *A Confederacy of Dunces* revolves around Reilly, who takes the opportunity to unleash his blistering manifesto about the pitfalls of modern humanity at every possible moment and cannot hold down the simplest job. From a Lucky Dog vendor to working in a textile factory, the smallest amount of responsibility is met with his indignation and egocentrism. The satirical novel includes a menagerie of memorable New Orleans characters, creating an engrossing observation of New Orleans culture. Unfortunately, Toole was never able to experience the success of his book.

Despondent over the lack of interest in his novel, in 1969 Toole killed himself. His mother Thelma became obsessed with having her son's novel published, but to no avail. Finally, she appealed to professor and novelist Walker Percy, who read the manuscript and persuaded Louisiana State University Press to publish it in 1980; it won the Pulitzer Prize for fiction in 1981.

In the early 1990s, hotel developer Pres Kabacoff believed that putting this "outrageous protagonist" in front of the hotel "made sense." The bronze statue created by local sculptor Bill Ludwig depicts Reilly in the opening of the book, standing in front of the former D. H. Holmes department store (now the Hyatt Centric) dressed in his signature hunting cap, baggy clothes, and scarf, holding a shopping bag and waiting for his mother while he studies the crowd for "signs of bad taste." Ludwig modeled the sculpture after actor and radio personality John "Spud" McConnell, who has portrayed Reilly multiple times in local theaters. In good taste, the sculpture is typically brought inside during Mardi Gras to avoid overzealous revelers.

Address 800 Iberville Street, New Orleans, LA 70130 | Tip John Kennedy Toole's grave is in Greenwood Cemetery. Visitors typically leave him copies of the book, pencils, and Lucky Dogs.

50 Immigrant Statues

Honoring the past and present

Between 1820 and 1860, New Orleans was the second-leading port of entry for immigrants behind New York City. Among these groups were Italians, Germans, Irish, Haitians, and Central European Jews. New Orleans' port was a major contributor to the city's growth, making it the largest city in the South in the 1850s. By the mid-1800s, more than half of the city's population was foreign-born.

While, typically, the French get most of the credit as the main ingredient for the city's cultural fusion, other ethnicities lend their customs to New Orleans' vibrant traditions. A surefire way to view these contributions is to witness the growth of diverse dance krewes, social organizations that participate in Carnival parades and balls. The Krewe da Bhan Gras was formed in 2022 to represent the South Asian diaspora in New Orleans, bringing Bollywood-style dance to the city's streets. The Krewe of PhantAsia represents the city's large Vietnamese and Filipino populations. Many members wear authentic clothing from Vietnam and the Philippines. The Lucha Krewe celebrates the heritage of Latin America and the Caribbean. Dancing exclusively to Latin music, the krewe mixes New Orleans masking traditions with the mascaras in Mexican lucha libre.

A more traditional way, however, to view New Orleans' cultural diversity year-round is represented through our statues. The *Monument to the Immigrant* statue was erected in 1995 and stands alongside the Mississippi River in Woldenberg Park. This marble monument by Franco Alessandrini portrays an immigrant family on one side, and on the other, a figure shaped like the bow of a ship.

In 2018, another sculpture was created by Alessandrini, this one mounted in Crescent Park to honor the Latinos who helped rebuild the city after the catastrophic effects of Hurricane Katrina. Standing 18 feet high in marble and bronze, the statue depicts Latinx men and women repairing the roof of a house, representing the thousands of homes that were rebuilt by these workers.

Address *Monument to the Immigrant* located by the Steamboat Natchez on the waterfront; the Latinx statue is near the Piety Street entrance to Crescent Park | Tip The *Molly Marine* statue, erected in 1943 and located at Elks Place, was the first statue of a woman in uniform in the United States, and is dedicated to women in the service.

51 Insta-Gator Ranch

A snappin' good time

In the 1970s, the American alligator was on the brink of extinction. There were fewer than 100,000 alligators in the state of Louisiana. Thanks to an innovative program from the Louisiana Department of Wildlife & Fisheries (LDWF), there are now almost 3 million alligators in the state, making it the largest population in the country. To put it in perspective, there are 4.5 million people in the state. For every couple, there are 1.3 alligators. But these creatures, which have been around for almost 37 million years, were rapidly diminishing around 50 years ago. The LDWF discovered that only six to eight percent of hatchlings survived in the wild. Its program involves harvesting alligator eggs from the wild and hatching them safely at local ranches. With human intervention, the survival rate is 85 percent. Of these alligators, approximately 10 to 17 percent are returned to the marsh once they reach an average size of four feet. The rest are used for their meat and skin. The initiative has been recognized as one of the most successful conservation programs in the country.

In 1989, John Price and his family opened the Insta-Gator Ranch & Hatchery; 12 years later, they opened it up to the public. It is one of 35 ranches in the state. The Insta-Gator Ranch offers an interactive, educational, and hands-on tour. And by hands-on, yes, you will be holding and touching alligators. The alligator "wranglers" take visitors through the history and anatomy of the alligator and its habitat in Louisiana. You can also view Bad Karma, a Nile crocodile with a grumpy disposition, and Bob, an alligator who is appropriately named because he is missing his tail. Another permanent resident is Blondie, a leucistic alligator, which means she has white or pale skin with blue eyes. You can also toss a marshmallow (one of their favorite treats) to a tank of four-year-old alligators and even catch and hold a baby alligator in their swimming pool. On average, there are 2,000 alligators on the ranch at any one time, enough to guarantee a "snappin' good time."

Address 7645 Allen Road, Covington, LA 70435 | Hours Tours usually run Tue–Sat 11am & 2pm; spring and summer, additional 1pm tour on Sundays | Tip Don's Seafood in Covington serves fried alligator as well as boudin balls, zydeco shrimp tacos, and blackened redfish.

52_JAMNOLA

More than a photo op

As a child (and an adult), Jonny Liss was the one handing out happy-face stickers. "I have always been the person who wants to bring others joy," says Liss. As the co-founder and "Ambassador of Joy" of JAMNOLA, which stands for Joy, Art & Music – New Orleans, Liss continues his mission of spreading happiness to this day. Liss, a self-proclaimed live music fanatic, was aware of various immersive experiences popping up around the country. Most of them, according to Liss, were "frivolous" and had nothing to do with culture and little to do with learning. Liss, an impresario of imagination, had the idea to bring joy to New Orleans through "large doses of music and art." He and his partner Chad Smith worked in collaboration with Where Y'Art Works to create a vibrant cultural funhouse in the Bywater.

Created during the Covid pandemic, and despite many challenges, JAMNOLA quickly became the city's cultural gem and outgrew its original space. It reopened in April 2025 on Frenchmen Street in the former historic Binder Bakery, which had closed in 2018. Twice the size of the original space at 10,000 square feet, every inch is thoughtfully and whimsically curated – despite the large area – to engage and engulf each visitor in 29 installations and 12 environments that revere the iconic art, music, cuisine, and traditions of New Orleans.

Walk through the belly of an alligator, jet into the future to see Mardi Gras Indians in space, explore the city's sewerage system, hang in an upside-down speakeasy, view a Mardi Gras float suspended in a tree, spend time in an Absinthe Garden, and visit 21 miniaturized historic music venues, many which have sound booths where you can listen to playlists curated by the renowned Melissa Weber, aka DJ Soul Sister.

All of this has been brought to life by over 100 local artists and collaborators, with 85 percent of the exhibits created using repurposed, reimagined, and recycled materials. At the end of your journey, you can choose to either exit the space by either "bouncing" or "second lining," ultimately leaving you with the equivalent of one giant happy-face sticker.

Address 940 Frenchmen Street, New Orleans, LA 70116 | Hours Mon 11am–4pm, Thu 2–7pm, Fri noon–8pm, Sat 10am–8pm, Sun 10am–6pm | Tip The Bywater Park was once a vacant lot and has been transformed by local artists into a charming park and sculpture garden.

53 Jazz Museum

Satchmo's cornet

The favorite son of New Orleans, Louis Armstrong, is synonymous with the city of his birth. A new permanent exhibition at the New Orleans Jazz Museum examines and demonstrates Armstrong's relationship with the city and how it inspired, changed, and challenged him.

Born into poverty in 1901 in "Jane Alley," to help earn money Armstrong spent his youth selling newspapers and delivering coal to Black Storyville prostitutes. After firing a gun on New Year's Eve, he was sent to the Municipal Waif's Home for Boys. With encouragement from the staff, Armstrong would learn discipline and be given a musical education, which would eventually take him around the world performing for sold-out crowds, royalty, heads of state, and for regular fixtures on radio, television, and the big screen. Although Armstrong eventually settled in Queens, New York, his heart was always in New Orleans, despite its Jim Crow laws making him simultaneously beloved and banished. From being named the King of Zulu in 1949 to a white announcer refusing to introduce him at a sold-out show, Armstrong struggled with the home that embraced and ostracized him.

The New Orleans Jazz Museum, judiciously located on the cusp of the French Quarter and the Frenchmen Street live music corridor, has the world's largest collection of instruments owned and played by seminal jazz musicians, including Louis Armstrong's cornet and bugle, Fats Domino's white Steinway piano, and Sidney Bechet's soprano saxophone. It also includes over 25,000 artifacts, including photographs, manuscripts, pictorial sheet music, recordings, and personal effects.

One of its main attractions is the frequent live music and theatrical performances offered. The museum's third floor is a state-of-the-art performance venue that hosts solo and small concerts, lectures, and interviews. The museum, with its interactive exhibits, research facilities, and live performances, honors the history of jazz in all its forms, and especially "Satchmo," the incomparable Louis Armstrong.

Address 400 Esplanade Avenue, New Orleans, LA 70116 | Hours Tue–Sun 9am–4pm | Tip The museum regularly offers free live-stream events of its productions, the next best thing to being there in person.

54 Kayaking on Bayou St. John

Paddle with nature

In most urban neighborhood Nextdoor or Facebook groups, it's common to have people post about stray dogs, loud neighbors, or dangerous potholes, but in Bayou St. John neighborhood groups, it's typical to post warnings about alligators. Although Bayou St. John, which is a navigable waterway, is not your typical place to find these reptiles, they do make frequent appearances. In 2021, a brave resident cut a six-footer free from a man-made trap on the banks. In 2023, a nine-foot alligator, who took to sunning himself on the banks of clover across from the post office and other spots on the bayou, was unceremoniously captured, thrown in the back of a truck, and rehomed to Maurepas Swamp. In 2024, a child standing in shallow water was bitten on the leg. There is no guarantee you'll spot a descendant of dinosaurs on Bayou St. John but it is something to watch for.

During Bayou Boogaloo, a weekend musical festival held every May, people lounge around in large inflatable unicorn floats or man-made watercraft, but the best way to experience Bayou St. John is by kayak or canoe.

Kayak-iti-Yat offers various tours, including custom group paddles from two to four hours that focus on the history and ecology of the area. You can learn while you paddle! Bayou Paddlesports offers kayak, canoe, and paddleboard rentals. They also have night paddles at sunset, Bayou Cleanup Day twice a year, and even dog days when your pooch is welcome into the watercraft.

Bayou St. John is one of the few places on earth you can paddle by an alligator as well as a West-Indies-style or French Colonial home, streetcar, or an all-girls Catholic school. Remember, despite making appearances on the bayou and on the sunny banks of clover, an alligator should never be tied to a fire hydrant in New Orleans. It is illegal. Seriously.

Address Bayou St. John, www.kayakitiyat.com, www.bayoupaddlesports.com | Hours Bayou accessible 24 hours; see websites for kayaking tours | Tip Many locals consider Parkway Bakery and Tavern, right off the bayou, the best place for po'boys. Hop in your kayak while enjoying a fried oyster or roast beef po'boy.

55 Kenner Planetarium and MegaDome Cinema

Space travel, Louisiana style

Located approximately 20 minutes outside of New Orleans is a space science complex that features a NASA International Space Station prototype, interactive weather exhibit, hands-on science center, and a theater for an out-of-this-world experience for any explorer. The MegaDome Cinema houses a 50-foot domed screen with stadium seating for 118 people, and screens films based on science and astronomy, planetarium star projection shows, and a variety of music laser shows.

The high-tech science area is extremely hands-on, with a multitude of devices that are not only entertaining but educational. Visitors can play a Laser Harp, Laze-O-Phone, and a theremin, an electronic musical instrument that is controlled without physical contact by the performer. There is also a digging station, where you can dig up dinosaur "fossils" with brushes and match them to a chart to explain what they are: Tyrannosaurus Rex Foot Claw, an Edmontosaurus Tooth Row, Brachiosaurus Thumb Claw, to name just three. One of the most innovative exhibits features a fly mask, where individuals can put on a steampunk-esque mask and look at the world through a fly's eyes.

The adjacent area is a full-scale prototype of NASA's International Space Station. There are multiple models to show the scale of an average-sized human next to a space station. Additionally, models of various spacecraft, including SpaceX's Starship, Space Launch System, and Orion, are placed throughout. A live weather station has also been set up from the International Space Station. There are multiple gadgets, robots, and informational placards that explore the history of NASA rocketry, and a hallway with a chronological timeline of space. The most intriguing aspect, however, is walking through the interior of the prototype. On display are the equipment worn by astronauts, examples of food they eat and how it is packaged, and what it is like to walk through a space station. All of this offers a visit to the galaxy here in Louisiana.

Address 2020 4th Street, Kenner, LA 70062 | Hours Tue–Fri 11am–4pm; groups, schools and camps must book ahead | Tip Rivertown Theaters for Performing Arts, located right around the corner, is an award-winning theater, staging 15 shows a year, including musicals and children's productions.

56 Laborde Mountain

A mountain for everyone

New Orleans, which sits on the banks of the Mississippi River, is famously located below sea level. The average elevation for the city is between one and two feet below sea level, with the lowest part being approximately eight feet under. But nestled deep in City Park is Couturie Forest, the city's highest peak and its own Mount Everest, Laborde Mountain. New Orleans' own epic mountain stands, according to the park's website, at a whopping 27 feet tall. The website cheekily mentions that they can supply oxygen tanks and sherpas on request.

Couturie Forest is named after Rene Couturie, an early City Park Improvement Association board member, who asked in his will that part of the park be preserved as a forest. Couturie gave the park $50,000, and in 1938 the site was dedicated and the first trees planted. Today, the 60-acre forest is dense with tree growth and a tranquil respite and refuge for city dwellers who double as nature lovers. Ranked one of the top birdwatching destinations in New Orleans with over 40 different types of birds, the area is also home to eight different ecosystems filled with over 60 types of trees, native plants, a lagoon, and diverse wildlife.

Despite being in the middle of a natural forest, Laborde Mountain is not natural; it is man-made. Dedicated in 2001 to the memory of Ellis P. Laborde, the former City Park general manager (1950–1978), the mountain is constructed from material and debris excavated from the construction of Interstate 610 in the 1970s. The trail is covered with woodchips and broken pieces of brick, and is probably the only mountain in the world where you will find oyster shells mixed in with the dirt. For your efforts, once you reach the summit of Laborde Mountain, you are rewarded with a small, slightly worn-down walk-in amphitheater, a stone-carved map of the area south of Lake Pontchartrain, and the deep satisfaction that only comes with breathing in the rarified air from the top of a mountain!

Address Located in Couturie Forest, 1 Palm Drive, New Orleans, LA 70124 | Hours Accessible 24 Hours | Tip Acorn: a Dickie Brennan & Co. Café is located in City Park overlooking the "Little Lake." This casual café offers local ingredients (including herbs from the Children's Museum's edible garden) to create updated versions of classic New Orleans fare.

57 Lakefront Airport

An Art Deco museum masquerading as an airport

Originally known as the Shushan Airport, this building has undergone as many makeovers as a Louisiana politician. Named after Abraham Shushan, President of the Board of Commissioners of the Orleans Levee District, the airport, which opened in 1934, was a groundbreaking facility – the world's first combined land and seaplane airport. It was also the largest and one of the most luxurious and highly rated airports in the country. It had, among other things, an AA-I rating, the U.S. Department of Commerce's highest rating, a 3,000-foot-long field, tennis courts, swimming pool, post office, surgical suite, and hotel-style rooms. One Navy flier compared its grandeur to that of the Grand Canyon. It was the essence of modernity with its Art Deco design, murals depicting flights in aviation history by Spanish artist Xavier Gonzalez, and statues and friezes by Enrique Alferez, whose sculpture *Fountain of the Four Winds* featuring four allegorical nude figures created a national incident. Those outraged by the nudity threatened to remove the male sculpture's genitals. Eleanor Roosevelt intervened, declared it art, and the statue and all its parts remained intact.

However, tragedy and scandal soon followed its triumphant debut. Amelia Earhart stopped there in May 1937 during her transatlantic flight. A little over a month later, her plane disappeared. Senator Huey P. Long, who aggressively backed the airport, was assassinated in 1935, and its namesake Shushan was convicted of wire fraud in 1941; subsequently, the airport was renamed Lakefront Airport. The building of the Moisant Field in 1946 (later renamed Louis Armstrong International Airport) became the city's main commercial airport. It underwent a $17 million renovation following Hurricane Katrina after more than four feet of water flooded the building.

The airport retains its multi-functional spirit as an active airport, flight school, popular venue destination, and living museum with its frescos, vintage telephone booths, and terrazzo floor that features a compass whose needles point to flight destinations around the world.

Address 6001 Stars and Stripes Boulevard, New Orleans, LA 70126 | Hours Mon–Fri 7am–5pm, Sat & Sun 8am–3pm | Tip The Runway Café in the airport offers daily breakfast and lunch specials, including a "Blue Plate Special," and an unparalleled view of the planes.

58 LaLaurie Mansion

The house of unspeakable horrors

On the corner of Royal and Governor Nicholls Streets is a three-story antebellum mansion that stands out from other residences in the French Quarter, not for its elaborate design but because of its dark history. Known as the LaLaurie Mansion, tourists come by nightly on tours to hear stories (some of them dubious) of the barbarous crimes committed behind the walls. The television show *American Horror Story: Coven* further ignited interest in what is known as one of the country's most haunted houses.

Delphine Macarty LaLaurie was a wealthy white woman born in New Orleans in 1787. She was married thrice, first at the age of 13, to a 35-year-old man after a scandalous affair. Widowed with children after her first two marriages, she married her third husband – a recent medical graduate, Dr. Louis LaLaurie, 16 years her junior. Rumors of her vicious treatment of her enslaved people had circulated in the city for years, and she was charged and fined for their mistreatment.

On April 10, 1834, a fire erupted in her home. Neighbors, concerned about her enslaved people – as it was whispered at the time that the upstairs of their home was used as a "prison" – broke the doors down, and much to everyone's horror, discovered seven enslaved persons of varied ages in numerous states of torture and mutilation.

Demanding justice, citizens stood in the streets awaiting Delphine's arrest. Suddenly, Delphine stepped from her house, into her awaiting carriage, and bolted. The outraged crowd almost destroyed the house. Delphine escaped to Paris, where she died and lay buried until her children had her remains exhumed and secretly brought back to be buried in her family's grave in St. Louis Cemetery No. 1. When her son-in-law sold her estate, including the enslaved, 19 of them were unaccounted for, which has nefarious implications. Over the years, the building has had multiple uses, including as a girls' school and tenement house, all with strange paranormal activity reported. Today, it is a personal residence and is the former home of actor Nicolas Cage.

Address 1140 Royal Street, New Orleans, LA 70116 | Tip To date, the only property Nicolas Cage still retains in New Orleans is his pyramid tomb in St. Louis Cemetery No. 1.

59 Latitude 29

Tiki renaissance

Donn Beach, considered the "founding father" of Tiki culture, was born in New Orleans in 1907 and popularized the Tiki movement in the 1930s. So, it's serendipitous that Jeff "Beachbum" Berry, universally hailed as the resurrector of the Tiki culture, would open a bar in New Orleans.

Growing up in Los Angeles in the 1960s, Berry fell in with the Polynesian culture. When the Tiki culture went the way of disco, and the country lapsed into what Berry describes as the "dark ages of the cocktail" in the 1980s, with wine coolers and white wine spritzers, Berry became determined to learn how to make the original Tiki recipes he loved. He quickly learned that Tiki recipes in the bar world equated to libation espionage. When he located some of Beach's recipes, he discovered they were in code. Berry spent years deciphering them and tracking down some of the original bartenders to unlock their secrets. Berry wasn't interested in running a bar at the time, he just wanted to drink his beloved Polynesian concoctions. Instead, he published booklets and pamphlets with the lost recipes, revealing the complexity and art form of these misunderstood drinks. In 2005, when he was invited to the Tales of the Cocktail and visited New Orleans for the first time, he and his wife Annene Kaye fell in love with the city. In 2014, they opened Latitude 29 and have been bringing the "aloha bartending and vibe" to the Crescent City ever since.

Latitude 29 is intimate, with only about 70 seats. Berry prides himself on his staff and his "Southern Pacific Cuisine," which includes oyster rumaki salad and fried Louisiana catfish. The décor primarily consists of Berry's personal collection and original artwork from Bosko Hrnjak, who designed the fish-trap lamps and all of the wood carvings, each of them unique. The drink menu, of course, features some of the recipes Berry unearthed, but also some unique to his restaurant. There's even a delicious Tiki Teetotalers section. Thanks to Berry, Latitude 29 is an oasis of the Tiki renaissance in New Orleans.

Address 321 N. Peters Street, New Orleans, LA 70130 | Hours Sun–Tue & Thu 3–10pm, Fri & Sat noon–11pm | Tip For a bar that serves the New Orleans classics, Peychaud's on Toulouse Street is the choice with Sazeracs, Vieux Carrés, Ojen Frappes, Peychaud's Fizz, Hurricanes, and Roffignacs.

60_Le Petit Theatre

The show goes on

Located just off Jackson Square, Le Petit Theatre Du Vieux Carré is New Orleans' most historic (and according to some, most haunted) playhouse. The theatre was established in 1916 and has operated at its current location since 1922. At that time, *Drama* magazine wrote that even though the French Quarter was a "smelly tumble-down district with narrow streets and shabby-genteel iron balconied apartments of antebellum days," the "spirit" of the actors was the finest they had ever seen, especially compared to the "patronizing manner of the diamond circle of New York and Chicago." Perhaps the troupe's camaraderie was due in part to dealing with the various apparitions.

The original structure was destroyed by fire in 1794. It was rebuilt a few years later in the Spanish Colonial style and was used by Union General Benjamin Butler as barracks for the army during the Civil War. Many have reported seeing Union soldiers walking the halls or hearing their scuffing boots. The most tragic ghost is a woman who fell (or was pushed) on the way to a romantic rendezvous from the catwalk to her death. Her ghost is said to walk the catwalk, particularly at night. The least popular spirit is an ex-manager who, it was alleged, killed himself in his office. Staff have reported feeling his angry gaze or have heard noises of slamming drawers and doors.

Despite these ghostly intrusions, Le Petit offers, for the living, scaled-down Broadway musicals, Pulitzer-prize-winning plays, operas, one-person shows and local productions. However, in 2009, the small theater faced severe financial hardships with a large mortgage and over $1 million in needed repairs. In 2011, the theater sold 60 percent of the building to restaurateur Dickie Brennan. Le Petit retained ownership of the original stage and dressing rooms. The two businesses now share lobby space and the theater's center courtyard. There was some controversy over the sale, with some people for and others against it, but through all of it, one thing rang true: "The show must go on." And it did, for both the living and the deceased.

Address 616 St. Peter, New Orleans, LA 70116 | **Hours** Vary based on the production | **Tip** The restaurant in the Le Petit is Tableau, a French Creole restaurant with multiple dining areas, including balcony seating with one of the best views of the French Quarter.

61 Lee Harvey Oswald's Haunts

Killer real estate

Four United States Presidents have been assassinated. One of the assassins was born right here in New Orleans.

Lee Harvey Oswald is most linked to Dallas, Texas where, on November 22, 1963, he shot and killed the 35th President, John F. Kennedy, and was himself killed two days later by nightclub owner Jack Ruby. But Oswald was born in New Orleans, and over his life of 24 years, Oswald lived in at least nine different houses in the city.

He was born in 1939 at the old French Hospital two months after his father's death. His first home was 2109 Alvar Street in the Upper Ninth Ward (which is now a vacant lot). His mother Marguerite Oswald moved the family around, until relocating them into half of a double at 831 Pauline Street in the Bywater. They later moved to 111 Sherwood Forest Drive near City Park. Between 1944 and 1953, the family lived in Covington in Louisiana, Dallas, and New York City. They returned to New Orleans in 1954, and lived in two apartments in the Garden District at 1452 and 1454 St. Mary Street. Oswald dropped out of school shortly before his 16th birthday. He later took an apartment at 126 Exchange Place in the French Quarter. A neighbor remembered him as a shy boy who always held the door for her. Oswald joined the Marines when he was 17 and received a hardship discharge in 1959; a month later, he went to the Soviet Union and applied for citizenship. He returned to the United States in June 1962 with wife Mariana and young daughter June.

The New Orleans house most associated with Oswald is 4905 Magazine Street, where he lived from May until September 1963 in a small mother-in-law apartment on the right side with his family. They moved out without notice and headed to Dallas where, two months later, he would be forever linked to the murder of a president. Ironically, the building is now a law office.

Hours Houses viewable from the outside only | **Tip** Le Bon Temps, an iconic bar and live music venue, is down the street from Oswald's last residence, and he allegedly hung out here and listened to music. There is a booth with a small, faded plaque that reads, *Lee Harvey Oswald Sat Here*.

62 Magnolia Bridge

Pathway to the past

Bayou St. John is the site of Louisiana's oldest settlement, founded a decade before the city itself. Originally, it was a trade route used by the Native American tribes, who showed early explorers and settlers that the bayou, along with a short portage, made for a "shortcut" around the often treacherous and unpredictable Lower Mississippi River. There is a path of travel from the Gulf of Mexico through the Rigolets, Lake Pontchartrain, and into the bayou that brings vessels less than two miles from the Mississippi River. The route saves almost 100 miles of mercurial upstream travel. The bayou's access to the river gave the city much of its strategic value.

Today, the main attraction on the bayou is the Magnolia Bridge. The large steel bridge dates to the late 19th century and originally pivoted at the center to allow commercial vessels and barges to pass. Prior to the 1970s, the bridge was used for vehicular traffic, but it is now only for pedestrians and bicyclists. It was refurbished in 2019 and painted a (sometimes controversial) bright blue.

When the bridge was first built, citizens flocked to it for a variety of reasons, including a duel in 1878. Two men, their seconds, and a surgeon met on the bridge with revolvers and bowie knives to settle their dispute. It was agreed that if the matter wasn't settled with their pistols, they would finish it with knives. After arguing over the brand of pistols, they were spotted by the police and ordered to stop. Also during this time, it was a frequent meeting place for St. John's Eve events on June 23, commemorating the birth of John the Baptist. Voodoo Priestess Marie Laveau held elaborate feasts on the bayou's banks. The tradition continues today and, typically, a shrine for Laveau is set up on the bridge; participants are asked to wear all white and bring offerings such as food, hair ribbons, candles, and flowers. The bridge, however, is primarily used as a place to watch the sunset, gather with friends, and even the occasional wedding ceremony. Centuries later, it still connects people.

Address Harding Drive, New Orleans, LA 70119 | Hours Accessible 24 hours | Tip The Pitot House located on the bayou is named for one of its owners, James Pitot, the first mayor of the incorporated city of New Orleans. It is the only colonial Creole country house in New Orleans that is open to the public and available for tours.

63 Margaret Place

Friend of orphans

In the early 19th century, it was difficult to be Irish in the United States. Margaret Haughery, born in Ireland in 1813, emigrated to Maryland with her parents and three of her six siblings when she was five years old. The older siblings were left behind to be sent for later. Margaret, however, never saw them again. In 1822, a yellow fever epidemic killed her parents and her sister. It is unknown what happened to her brother, but at the age of nine, Margaret lost her entire family and was in a strange country alone. She became a domestic servant for a family to earn her keep and in 1835, she married Charles Haughery and moved to New Orleans. They eventually had a daughter, but tragedy continued to follow Margaret, and within a short time, her husband and daughter died of disease. She was alone again and in a strange place, but the Sisters of Charity, a community of Catholic nuns, gave her a place to live and helped her find a job as a laundress. Margaret donated as much as two-thirds of her salary to help the orphans in the nuns' care and used her savings to buy two cows, so she could provide them with fresh milk. Although she was illiterate, Margaret was a savvy businesswoman, and those two cows expanded into a thriving dairy. Next, she invested in a failing bakery and transformed it into the largest bakery in the United States.

Known simply as "Margaret," she never forgot the orphans (she personally built multiple orphanages) or the poor, and each day would deliver any leftover product to them.

Margaret became ill in 1882 and received a crucifix and blessing from the Pope. When she died, she was given a state funeral; mayors and governors were her pallbearers. A street in the Lower Garden District was named after her, and a statue was erected in her honor. It was only the second public statue dedicated to a woman in the United States and the first to a female businesswoman. She left her entire estate to the orphans of New Orleans.

Address 1142 Margaret Place, New Orleans, LA 70130 | Tip The luxury boutique St. Vincent Hotel was originally the St. Vincent's Infant Asylum, founded by Margaret.

64 Marie Laveau's Home

Voodoo priestess

A house on St. Ann Street is the location where perhaps one of the most misunderstood historical figures once lived – Voodoo Priestess Marie Laveau. During her lifetime, and for over 100 years after her death, Laveau's life was draped in layers of legend and mythology.

Born in 1801 to an unmarried free woman of color and married at age 18 to Jacques Parish, Laveau was "widowed" three years later in what eventually turned out to be abandonment. Shortly after, Laveau started a relationship with white businessman Christoper Glapion. The couple had seven children together, all of whom were raised in the same house that Laveau was.

Originally owned by Laveau's grandmother Catherine Henry, the cottage, built around 1798, was described as a low-roofed, four-roomed Creole cottage with a heavily tiled roof that was obscured behind a high fence. Marie Dede, who used to play with Laveau's grandchildren, recalled that children were not allowed in the front room because it was used for services, describing it as having many altars covered with flowers, pictures of saints, and burning candles.

One of Laveau's ceremonies involved placing a statue of St. Anthony, the patron saint of lost and stolen articles, upside down in her yard to find missing items or return wayward lovers. Her community value was demonstrated in 1871, when the church's sexton entered Greenwood Cemetery early in the morning to find someone as pale as the "salt sea foam" in a sheet with shaggy "demons" dancing around. The sexton fled and called the police, who sent for Laveau to exorcise the demons. It was later discovered to be a group of drunken men, but it demonstrates her esteem in being summoned by the police for her help.

The cottage was torn down in 1903. A new house stands in its place, causing many to believe that Laveau's ghost still resides there – some have claimed to have seen her walking in a long white dress and tignon (turban). People frequently leave hair ties on the house's shutters as an offering since it was rumored she worked as a hairdresser.

Address 1020–1022 St. Ann Street, New Orleans, LA 70130 | Hours Viewable from the outside only | Tip The Healing Center (2372 St. Claude Avenue) has the International Shrine of Marie Laveau, where you can leave offerings and gifts to try and curry her favor.

65 Marigny Opera House

Artistic holy ground

The Holy Trinity Church was established in 1853 in the historic Marigny neighborhood by its largely German Catholic population. Like other New Orleans neighborhoods, immigrants tended to settle in areas by ethnic group and establish their own community. The Holy Trinity Church was in the middle of the area nicknamed "Little Saxony," or the *Faubourg des Allemands*, a German suburb, because of its large German population. While New Orleans didn't follow the typical puritanical Sunday customs of most American cities, the Germans' "excessive carousing" was shocking on this holy day of the week even by their standards. After church, Germans visited friends, played cards, and danced and drank their Sunday nights away in the beer gardens.

The Holy Trinity Church remained for over 150 years until dwindling attendance caused it to close in 1997. The ground was deconsecrated, and the church went up for sale. Its transformation was nothing short of miraculous. Left empty for years, the building was damaged during Hurricane Katrina in 2005. In 2011, it was purchased by Dave Hulbert and Scott King, who turned it into a performing arts and event venue and renamed it the Marigny Opera House. The non-denominational "Church of the Arts" opened in November 2011 for the Fringe Festival. Since then, the 3,000-square-foot space, with its restored bell tower, cupola roof, and 120-plus-year-old stained glass windows, has hosted a myriad of events. Solange Knowles and Alan Ferguson were married in the former church, and Depeche Mode filmed a music video there. In 2014, the Marigny Opera Ballet was created, and it performs multiple times during the year. You can also catch classic theater here, such as a Tennessee Williams play, chamber music, aerial shows set to jazz, Afro-Brazilian music, variety shows, and of course, opera. The space is also used for private and corporate events, and won a Preservation Award from the Louisiana Landmark Society.

Address 725 St. Ferdinand Street, New Orleans, LA 70117 | Hours Vary based on the event | Tip If you are interested in repurposed buildings, the Engine 24 Firehouse Bed & Breakfast is in a former early 20th-century firehouse.

66__Maya Snorkel

Swim with stingrays

The Audubon Aquarium is consistently ranked one of the top five aquariums in the country. Located adjacent to the Mississippi River in the French Quarter, the aquarium transports you to distinct habitats, from the Louisiana swamps and bayous to central and southern Mexico and the Caribbean.

In the Down the Bayou exhibit, you can visit Tchompitoulas (nicknamed "Chomps"), the leucistic alligator raised from a hatchling. The all-white alligator, who most people mistakenly identify as an albino, is often thought to be a statue, not just for his shocking fluorescent blue eyes but for his general lazy demeanor. In the Gulf exhibit, you can meet King Midas. This octogenarian green turtle, who shares a 400,000-gallon tank with sharks, stingrays, and schools of fish, is a notorious show-off and likes to keep the staff company when they clean the tanks. The Amazon exhibit takes you into the Amazon-Orinoco rainforest with piranhas, pacu fish, and tropical birds flying overhead. There are also nearly two-dozen African penguins, a jellyfish gallery, and a touch tank. When there is the staffing capacity, guests can also feed cownose rays.

The stunner is the Great Maya Reef tunnel, a 4,200-square-foot, 30-foot-long tunnel that finds you surrounded by stingrays and vibrant tropical fish found in the Gulf of Mexico and the Mesoamerican Reef, such as longjawed squirrelfish, saucereye porgy, and blue tangs. The real experience, however, is to become part of the exhibit itself. At certain times, the Maya Snorkel Adventure allows a maximum of four people to swim in the tunnel. After a brief snorkel and safety lesson, guests can swim amongst the aquatic inhabitants. "One of the coolest things we do with the snorkelers," says Michael Penninga, the Assistant Dive Safety Officer, "is interact with the guests who are walking through the tunnel." Penninga loves waving to the small children, who are often so amazed they topple over. This remarkable experience also helps fund conservation efforts in the actual Mesoamerican Reef.

Address 1 Canal Street, New Orleans, LA 70130 | Hours Daily 10am–5pm; Maya Snorkel Adventure Fri & Sat 12:30pm | Tip The calliope on the Steamboat Natchez, located on the Mississippi River, plays almost every day around 11am and then later in the afternoon.

67 Mayfair House

Witches and demons

Before AMC's *Mayfair Witches* television series, a supernatural horror/fantasy drama series inspired by novelist Anne Rice's trilogy, this marquis mansion on Prytania Street was primarily known as the Soria-Creel House. Its remarkable history started in 1845 when Winnifred Hubbard, a free woman of color, purchased nine lots in what was then the city of Lafayette. The lots comprised almost an entire city block. Seven years later, Lafayette was annexed by the city of New Orleans, and in 1868, businessman Cohen Soria purchased a subdivided lot from Hubbard and built a two-storied, double-galleried side hall Italianate-style house with Doric posts, four-over-four full-length windows, and an arched entrance. In 1991, Terry and Elizabeth Hadden Creel purchased the home from descendants of Soria and converted it from a double- into a single-family residence.

In the TV series, the home exudes a sense of hazy foreboding: it is weathered with patina, and the only color is the pink roses carelessly punctuating the seemingly eternal mist. In reality, this lightly pastel-colored house is gracefully surrounded by sago palms and live oaks and invokes an understated refinement. But while this may be the visual representation of the *Mayfair Witches* house, it wasn't the inspiration.

Anne Rice used her own sprawling, antebellum two-story Italianate-Greek-Revival-hybrid home on 1239 First Street as inspiration for the *Mayfair Witches* house. Located just nine blocks away from the television house, Rice's home is known as the Rosegate Home, for the fence containing elegant rosettes. Rice used her advance from *The Witching Hour* to purchase the house, and in a 2014 Facebook post, wrote that she made her home into the Mayfair family of witches, and it was figured into five of her novels. The first sentence of *The Witching Hour* mentions this house, and the home remains a central character through her Mayfair works. Both homes demonstrate how architecture can awaken inspiration and even the supernatural.

Address 3102 Prytania Street, New Orleans, LA 70115 | Hours Viewable from the outside only | Tip The Garden District Book Shop has a large collection of first editions signed by Anne Rice.

68 Miss Claudia's Vintage Clothing & Costumes

Stylish home of "Ain't There No Mo"

Step inside Miss Claudia's Vintage Clothing & Costumes, and your vision will instantly be filled with decades of eclectic vintage pieces: 1920s beaded-sheath dresses, 1940s men's silk smoking jackets, 1960s go-go dresses, 1970s powder-blue leisure suits, and 1980s poofy-sleeved pastel prom gowns. Owned by local actor and singer Claudia Baumgarten, Miss Claudia's is the oldest non-corporate vintage and costume shop in New Orleans run by a sole proprietor. While her shop primarily carries Southern vintage and showcases labels from New Orleans stores that "Ain't There No Mo," such as D. H. Holmes and Maison Blanche, the store is a purveyor of all things vintage and all things fun. Digging through her clothing racks, you are likely to find everything from velvet opera capes to old letterman jackets, to a 1950s sheer pink-lace pleated tulle party dress that harks back to Grace Kelly.

After Hurricane Katrina, so many new grassroot krewes sprung up to celebrate New Orleans culture that Baumgarten expanded her costume selection to accommodate them. While it's typical of many New Orleanians to have a "costume closet," you don't need to have an entire space dedicated to the art of dressing up to be able to find room for a few vibrantly colored wigs, rhinestone jewelry, glittery platform boots, colorful tights and tutus, or unusual collectible cuff-links. Aside from costume components for Halloween and Mardi Gras, you can also pick up a flowered headpiece for Day of the Dead, lederhosen for Oktoberfest, and a green top hat for St. Patrick's Day. And if you're unsure exactly what look you're striving for, bring in your ideas, and the staff, who "specialize in imagination," will help you put together the perfect ensemble. Baumgarten says that her clientele ranges from the bohemian to the conservative, proof that costuming in New Orleans is truly egalitarian.

Address 4204 Magazine Street, New Orleans, LA 70115, www.missclaudias.com | Hours Mon–Sat 10am–6pm, Sun noon–5pm | Tip Uptown Costume & Dancewear on 4326 Magazine Street has a large selection of costumes, wigs, hats, and dancewear.

69 Mr. Bingle

A hole in one

"Jingle, jangle, jingle, here comes Mr. Bingle." Any child in New Orleans in the late 1940s through the early 1980s was familiar with this little ditty. It meant Christmas was coming. Created in 1947 by Emile Alline, a window display manager of the department store Maison Blanche, Mr. Bingle was a snowman Santa Claus brought to life to become his helper. After the snowman expressed the desire to fly, Santa gave him holly wings. He also gifted him with blue ornaments for eyes and an upside-down ice cream cone for a hat. The little snowman was named Mr. Bingle (the same initials as the department store). At first, he was just an illustration in advertisements, but when he became a puppet at the hands of Edwin "Oscar" Isentrout, he became a local sensation.

Isentrout was a German immigrant and puppeteer who performed puppet shows under the bill "Oscar and the Little Woodenheads" at burlesque clubs on Bourbon Street, with showgirl marionettes who stripped down to display little lightbulbs on their chests. Isentrout and his team performed multiple Mr. Bingle puppet shows a day at Maison Blanche from Thanksgiving until Christmas. Isentrout, whose high-pitched voice provided a child-like quality, would have Mr. Bingle get into various misadventures from which Santa would rescue him. Mr. Bingle eventually got his own television show, which was also broadcast on the radio and performed live in the store windows. Since Istentrout died in 1984, Mr. Bingle has remained silent.

There are many tributes to Mr. Bingle around the city, but one of the most endearing is at City Putt, a 36-hole miniature golf course in City Park. There are two courses. The Louisiana Course highlights festivals around the state, and the New Orleans Course showcases iconic local themes – including the beloved Mr Bingle, who continues to bring the spirit of Christmas to visitors year-round.

Address City Putt, 33 Dreyfuss Drive, New Orleans, LA 70119 | Hours Wed–Fri 3–9pm, Sat & Sun 10am–9pm | Tip Celebration in the Oaks is a light festival in City Park that begins after Thanksgiving and continues until shortly after the New Year. It also features a giant fiberglass statue of Mr. Bingle.

70__Ms. Mae's

Cheap drinks and cool bathrooms

Let's be perfectly clear: Ms. Mae's is not the place to get craft cocktails or fine wine. Do not expect the bartenders to be in a uniform and dazzle you with a fancy sleight of hand as they pour your multi-ingredient cocktail and garnish it with a piece of fruit carved to look like a flower. Ms. Mae's is widely known for three things: cheap drinks, opening 24 hours, and being cash only.

The drinks are standard, a basic wells cocktail is $3, and a double is $4. It's a $2 upcharge for something as "sophisticated" as Red Bull or ginger beer. Everywhere in the bar there are signs to remind you it is cash only and you'll pay a hefty penalty if you attempt to pay with a credit card. Such signs include: Satan threatening your "perverted soul" to an eternity of fire, the Incredible Hulk threatening to "smash dat ass," and a photo of Samuel L. Jackson with the words, "CASH ONLY MF'ER!" To reiterate, it is CASH ONLY.

For decades, the bar located on the prime corner of Magazine Street and Napoleon Avenue has been the late-night haunt of many. There is both the typical pool table and air hockey table, built-in wooden booths, and a scattering of chairs and tables. The patio in the back is new, allowing for some fresh air, but even with that, time manages to stand still in Ms. Mae's due to its purposefully low-light atmosphere. What it lacks in a designer's curated touch, it makes up for in its bathrooms – four of them to be exact. One is dedicated to pinups, with multiple photographs of 1950s glamour girls in a diamond pattern. Another is an homage to Mardi Gras, with tiles of various Mardi Gras Krewes. The third is a tribute to Wonder Woman, with an entire wall of her cartoon image. And the fourth recognizes The Artist Formerly Known as Prince, in deep purple and black, with tiles displaying his personal symbol and a photo of him in the center. If you are up for the challenge, it is possible to reach legendary customer status at Ms. Mae's, but it does involve having one drink, every hour, for 24 hours. Those four bathrooms will come in handy.

Address 4336 Magazine Street, New Orleans, LA 70115 | Hours Daily 24 hours | Tip Peaches Record Store, located practically next door to Ms. Mae's, has been in existence for 50 years and is the best place to buy vinyl and discover new upcoming artists.

71 Music Box Village

Imagination invitation

In the middle of a space that is a fusion between a shanty town and miniaturized corrugated metal Roman coliseum, lies a series of structures that look like they were dreamed up by the likes of Howard Roark and Dr. Seuss. The Music Box Village, operated by the nonprofit New Orleans Airlift, which works to forge cultural connections through collaborative artworks, has been a place of musical wonder in the Bywater for over 10 years. Initially in different spaces, this ever-changing and evolving outdoor venue is an ongoing experiment in "musical architecture." There are over a dozen "musical houses" that pulsate with sound at every touch, hit, strike, or slap. The houses are sensory wonders, embracing the visual, tactile, and auditory. During operating hours, visitors can strike drums with mallets, strum the guitar-string railings, tug on ropes for chimes, stomp on metal steps, or even take off their shoes and slap the pipes. They can sing or talk through the receiver in a vintage phone booth and have their voice broadcast across the Village, or harmonize with the bars of a giant birdcage with a large bald eagle inside, or literally play the Les Paul House.

Christian Repaal, the builder and art fabricator at the Village, has been working with artists all over the world to create unique structures that stimulate visitors visually and musically. "We will sometimes build and rebuild things dozens of times, especially musical components before we get it right," Repaal laughs, "and that's okay because the artists might not have engineering degrees, and they aren't well-versed in having their art hit with sticks."

The goal of the Village is to gather communities. At night, the space takes on an almost phantasmagorical quality with lights draped across the different sculptures. Over the years, numerous musicians have played here, including acts such as Wilco, Norah Jones, Peaches, and the Preservation Hall Jazz Band. They can, according to Repaal, easily seat 1,000, but most shows average about 300 and there are no "bad seats."

Address 4557 N. Rampart Street, New Orleans, LA 70117, www.musicboxvillage.com | Hours Typically Sat & Sun, 10am–3pm (see website for events calendar) | Tip The Rabbit Hole on Oretha Castle Haley Boulevard is another great outdoor musical venue that hosts a variety of acts. The Grammy Award-winning Rebirth Brass Band plays a regular gig there every Tuesday night.

72 Musical Legends Park

Legends in bronze

Bourbon Street is notorious for its party reputation. Pounding music pulsates out of open doors with hawkers trying to cajole you inside, vibrant neon clashes with its wrought-iron balconies, and due to the open-container law, people walk the streets carrying their "Big-Ass Beers" and brightly colored cocktails, such as the Hurricane and the Hand Grenade. This 13-block street features restaurants, bars, souvenir shops, strip clubs, music venues, karaoke joints, and dance clubs. It's surprising to learn that the street is not named for the amber-colored alcohol but for a French royal family, the House of Bourbon. It's even more surprising that amongst all these establishments that advertise the excessive pursuit of pleasure, is nestled a park that was originally dedicated to inventor Thomas Edison.

The 44-foot by 127-foot area was an electricity substation park for more than 60 years. New Orleans Public Service, Inc. donated the park in the early 1970s and called it Edison Park. The site was adorned with trees and waterfalls, but the city failed to maintain it, and it fell into disrepair and was locked up. In 2001, it was converted into Musical Legends Park, a space that commemorates the city's musical heritage with life-sized bronze statues depicting famous local musicians.

Musical greats such as Irma Thomas, Louis Prima, Allen Toussaint, and Chris Owens are placed throughout the brick courtyard. Café Beignet sells beignets and croissants as well as other classic New Orleans fare, such as jambalaya, gumbo, and crawfish étouffée. There is also a small bar on the side that sells cocktails and frozen drinks. Located in the center is Pete's Wishing Well Fountain, dedicated to clarinetist Pete Fountain. Make a wish and toss in a coin, and you might make a wish come true for someone else as the money goes to providing McDonogh Elementary School with band equipment.

Starting at 10am, local musicians play. These performances are free and anyone can come in and listen (including dogs on leash), but the tables are generally reserved for those who order food and drink.

Address 311 Bourbon Street, New Orleans, LA 70130 | Hours Thu–Sun 8am–10pm, Mon 8am–3pm | Tip Fritzel's Jazz Club on Bourbon Street is the oldest continually operating jazz club on the street and has live music daily starting at 12:30pm.

73 Napoleon's Death Mask

A Spanish history

In New Orleans, the French military leader and emperor Napoleon Bonaparte is everywhere. One of the city's main thoroughfares is named after him. The Napoleon House bar and restaurant in the French Quarter is the former home of mayor Nicholas Girod (1751–1840). It is named as such because Girod plotted (unsuccessfully) to rescue Napoleon from his exile in St. Helena and bring him to New Orleans to stay in the house. And his death mask resides in The Cabildo museum.

The Cabildo, located next door to St. Louis Cathedral in Jackson Square, was built under Spanish rule between 1795 and 1799 and was the center of New Orleans government until 1853, when it became the headquarters of the Louisiana State Supreme Court. Finally, this exquisite Spanish colonial building was transferred to the Louisiana State Museum in 1908.

Napoleon's death mask has had about as many lives as the building that houses it. The bronze mask is one of nine original ones created by Napoleon's physician Dr. Francesco Antommarchi 40 hours after Napoleon's death on May 6, 1821. Antommarchi made the mask's mold from either wax or plaster, applying it to Napoleon's face. He used that mold to cast the bronze masks. When Antommarchi immigrated to New Orleans in 1834, he gave one to the city. It was first displayed at The Cabildo and then moved to Gallier Hall where, during renovations, it ended up in the trash. Former city treasurer Adam Giffen took the mask, displaying it in his home. It ended up with an antique dealer, who sold it to Captain W. G. Raoul. He donated it to the city, which gave the mask to the Louisiana Historical Society. They returned it to The Cabildo, its original home, over 75 years later.

The Cabildo, with its three floors of exhibitions – which cover the history of Louisiana through historical documents, paintings, weapons, maps and sculptures – is a historical treasure and a must-see.

Address 701 Chartres Street, New Orleans, LA 70116 | Hours Tue–Sun 9am–4pm | Tip The Presbytère, located on the same street, has two permanent exhibits: "Mardi Gras: It's Carnival Time in Louisiana" is dedicated to revelry; "Living with Hurricanes: Katrina and Beyond" tells of resilience and renewal.

74 New Orleans Craft Culture

Glitter by the pound

In New Orleans, crafting is not just a hobby but a way of life. And oh, what a life! NOLA Craft Culture uses this mantra as its theme. The owners, Lisette Constantin and Nori Pritchard, hold PhDs in Clinical Psychology and Biomedical Engineering respectively, and now put their efforts toward decorating New Orleans!

Hundreds of colors of glitter line the walls, as well as miles of fringe and trim, buckets of feathers and plumes, bowls of rhinestones and sequins, and jars of confetti with mermaids, flamingos, sharks, and more. And if your cheeks or eyes need a little more shimmer, NOLA Craft Culture also carries dozens of wearable glitter products from locally owned companies.

Being surrounded by all this sparkle might make you feel a bit overwhelmed. Not to worry! There are custom-made kits with all the supplies (and instructions) you need to paint, decorate, and gild oysters or construct tropical resin drinks from coconuts, just to name a few.

It's not just a craft store; it's also a community workspace and makerspace. Downstairs is the workshop where Glittering 101 classes are frequently offered, using locally named glitter colors such as Absinthe Hallucinations, Commander's Palace, and Louisiana Iris. Year-round classes are offered in Alcohol Ink Rainbow Glitter techniques, how to construct headpieces and fascinators, and glitter-transfer techniques. They also provide seasonal classes such as glittering pumpkins, making spooky headpieces, Mardi Gras masks, Easter bonnets, second line umbrellas, and reindeer antlers. If you are looking for a more customized experience, they host private crafting parties. According to Nori Pritchard, one of the best features of NOLA Craft Culture is that "visitors not only experience deeper appreciation for the local culture, but they can also reap the many social and emotional benefits of community and creative expression," and, as a bonus, take home something sparkly!

Address 127 S. Solomon Street, New Orleans, LA 70119 | Hours Tue–Sat 10am–6pm, Sun noon–6pm | Tip Elektra Cosmetics is a locally owned company that sells chunky glitter gels, face, and body shimmers, as well as a plant-based biodegradable glitter known as EKO Glitter.

75 Ninth Ward Memorial Arch

Controversial tribute to WWI

When the United States entered World War I on April 6, 1917, 74,103 Louisianians served in the military, primarily through the draft. It was the first war where women served, and 131 Louisiana women enlisted as Navy yeoman. When the Armistice was signed on November 11, 1918, the city had a huge celebration with impromptu parades and free-flowing alcohol. Immediately, there was a call to honor the veterans.

Dr. Edward S. Kelly, a Ninth Ward resident and prominent physician, organized a committee that raised $7,800 for the construction of a commemorative arch recognizing those in the ward who served in the war. The Ninth Ward at that time was a racially diverse neighborhood of working-class families that were predominantly born and raised in the city. The committee canvassed the neighborhood for donations and held multiple fundraisers. It was noted that "not one penny for the erection was solicited outside of the ward."

The granite arch, which was finished with marble, measured 28 feet tall, 21 feet wide, and 7 feet thick. It was completed in October 1919, but the dedication was delayed due to the completion of the bronze tablets.

The monument was dedicated on March 14, 1920, with over 6,000 in attendance. It was the first World War I memorial in the country. Over 1,200 names of Ninth Ward residents who served were inscribed on four bronze tablets: three honoring white men who served, and one honoring African American men who served. One woman's name, Frances Fabing, was listed. Fabing saw active service overseas with Base Hospital Unit 24 and had a prominent role at the dedication.

Recently, the segregation of the veterans' names moved people to call for the monument to be taken down. While it demonstrates that Black members were being remembered for their service, it shows that their fight for equality was far from over. At its best, it demonstrates the resolve and pride of a community working together to honor its own.

Address 3800 Burgundy Street, New Orleans, LA 70117 | Tip Another World War I monument is the bronze *Doughboy* statue in the greenspace at Tulane Avenue and South Galvez Street surrounded by the buildings of the new University Medical Center.

76_Orleans Gallery by Louisiana Art

Passion unparalleled

Cayman Clevenger saw his first piece of art, a Clementine Hunter painting entitled *Pecan Pickin'*, when he was three years old and living in Many, Louisiana. His neighbor, Julian Foy, was one of Hunter's earliest patrons, and he had invited Clevenger and his family over. The young Clevenger peppered Foy with questions about his art, and from then on, anytime Clevenger wanted to view said art, Foy's door was open. The experience was transformative for Clevenger. "She had a way of depicting the Louisiana landscape," Clevenger states, "that made me realize that I should truly appreciate the beauty in it and the world around it." Hunter depicted a hard life, but she was also painting the same sky that Clevenger saw, and it forced him to see the simple beauty in the real world the same way he sees it in a painting. Foy died when Clevenger was a tween, and he stated in his will that Clevenger could have first pick of his art and be able to purchase one piece at the price he paid for it. Clevenger chose *Pecan Pickin'*.

Clevenger, who has a degree in History and a minor in Art History, put himself through college and law school by selling art. He is the only attorney in Louisiana who is also a certified fine art appraiser.

In the spring of 2025, Clevenger fulfilled his childhood dream and opened his own gallery, Orleans Gallery by Louisiana Art, which specializes in local and regional art. Although he represents over 25 artists, including sculptors, potters, and mixed media, folk art is still Clevenger's first love. He frequently has shows that pair work by deceased artists with contemporary artists such as Walter Anderson and Adam Trest, and Clementine Hunter and Andrew LaMar Hopkins.

The 1,800-square-foot gallery is a piece of art itself with exposed bricks, large windows, and antique chandeliers. All of this allows the customer to see the beauty of art just as Clevenger first experienced it as a child.

Address 603 Julia Street, New Orleans, LA 70130 | Hours Wed–Sun 11am–6pm | Tip LeMieux Galleries, also located on Julia Street, is well known for its contemporary works by local artists of the Gulf Coast.

77 Our Lady of La Vang

East meets West

The thriving Vietnamese population in New Orleans (the largest in the state) celebrates Tết, the Vietnamese New Year, in grand style every year. Our Lady of La Vang Catholic Church in the Gentilly neighborhood was dedicated in 1992 and is named after the reported 1798 Virgin Mary apparition to persecuted Catholics in the Vietnamese town of La Vang. Thousands took refuge in the rainforest of La Vang in Quảng Trị Province. Starving and freezing, one night during their prayers, they were visited by a female apparition dressed in traditional Vietnamese clothes and holding a child in her arms with two angels beside her. The apparition told the refugees to boil tree leaves to cure themselves, which they did.

The blend of East and West is apparent at the La Vang shrine at the church in Gentilly. At the entrance to the gate on top of columns are Foo Dogs, also known as guardian lions or *nghê*. They are mythical lion-dog hybrids used as mascots in pagodas, shrines, and temples. The shrine is pagoda-style with a fleur-de-lis cross on top. Underneath the pagoda in the center is a traditional western interpretation of the Virgin Mary holding baby Jesus, but she is standing on a dome with a map of Vietnam. Around the shrine is an intricate metal fence featuring multiple circular symbols, including animals sacred to Vietnamese culture: Foo Dogs; dragons, a symbol of divinity and power; the phoenix, symbolizing virtue and rebirth; and turtles, symbolizing longevity and good fortune. One of the symbols is a map of Vietnam surrounded by multiple images of the Lac Bird, a mythical creature and national bird of Vietnam that symbolizes the desire to overcome challenges, and a version of the Kylan, another mythical creature which is the Vietnamese version of the unicorn and combines elements of the horse, buffalo, and dragon. The Vietnamese believe the kylan is powerful and faithful, perfect for guarding temples and places of worship. You might not be a believer, but you should feel the energy of this heavenly shrine.

Address 6054 Vermillion Boulevard, New Orleans, LA 70122 | Hours Viewable from main gate 24 hours | Tip New Orleans takes pride in its food, even in gas stations, and there is a whole side culture dedicated to it. Banh Mi Boys, named after Banh Mi, a Vietnamese po'boy, launched his restaurant in his family's gas station and it took off. Banh Mi Boys now has multiple locations in the city.

78 Painted Ladies

A Victorian trio

Scenic Esplanade Avenue is known for its 19th-century mansions, but a trio of colorful Italianate townhouses stand out. Originally built by cotton broker Julius Weiss in 1883 as spec townhouses for investment purposes, these three multi-colored houses each have their own unique architectural identities. The house at 2222 Esplanade is the only one considered real Italianate and is apartments; 2212 Esplanade has a Swiss cottage influence and is a private residence; 2216 Esplanade is a traditional Queen Anne building and is a boutique hotel, La Belle Esplanade. All three of the houses are as vibrant and unapologetic as their owner Matthew King.

King, a self-described "raconteur extraordinaire" from Connecticut, originally purchased 2212 Esplanade with his wife Melanie Schmitt. They eventually acquired all three buildings. King calls owning all of them "a blessing and a curse."

Every guest room of La Belle Esplanade is unique, with two rooms, a bath, and its own patio access. And like the buildings themselves, the rooms are all linked but all distinct. Each has a different theme, different color (walls and ceiling), and a different French name (*Clio, Les Fleurs,* and *Les Pêches*, for instance). The rooms are adorned with Mardi Gras and New Orleans memorabilia and various art from local artists, including from King himself, who did all the paintings.

King, who eats lunch out every day and is quick with recommendations, encourages his guests to leave the hotel and spend their days exploring the French Quarter and Treme, and to "live like a local." If by chance, however, you find yourself back at La Belle Esplanade in the afternoon, wander out to the back and visit with the chickens who are roaming the courtyard for their daily exercise. Just like the rooms, they have different names, just don't expect King to tell you which chicken is Goldie 1 and which one is Goldie 2. Visible from the courtyard is also a giant mural of a Mardi Gras Indian on the back of a neighboring house that is not visible from the street.

Address 2212, 2216, 2222 Esplanade Avenue, New Orleans, LA 70119 | Hours Viewable from the outside only | Tip Across the street on the corner is Gayarre Place, a small triangular park named after historian Charles Etienne Arthur Gayarre. The large monument called *Peace, the Genius of History* was originally on display at New Orleans' 1884 World's Industrial Cotton Centennial Exposition.

79_Parrothead Pilgrimage

Bubba as a busker

Jimmy Buffett, the singer-songwriter often associated with the laid-back tropical vibe of Key West, credits New Orleans for his start in music. On stage during his performance at the 2012 New Orleans Jazz & Heritage Festival, Buffett said, "This is where it all started. New Orleans was my Paris before I got to Paris."

Born in 1946 and graduating from the University of Southern Mississippi in 1969, Buffett moved to New Orleans, where he busked on the French Quarter streets and played at Bourbon Street bars, getting his musical education. In an interview Buffett said he didn't think there would be a Jimmy Buffett without New Orleans.

Aside from his multiple songs about New Orleans – "I Will Play For Gumbo," "City of New Orleans," "The Wino and I Know," "Breathe In, Breathe Out," and "The University of Bourbon Street" – Buffett was also an avid New Orleans Saints Fan and frequent headliner of the New Orleans Jazz & Heritage Festival.

In 2011, Garland Robinette painted Buffett for the Jazz Fest poster, portraying him busking as a young man on the corner of Royal and Dumaine Streets in the French Quarter in front of the iconic Miltenberger House, a ca. 1838 three-story Greek Revival building with cast-iron galleries and floor-to-ceiling windows. Parrotheads continue to this corner, typically dressed in their parrothead attire and take selfies.

Other places for avid Parrotheads are the Tropical Isle (721 Bourbon Street), famous for its cocktail the "Hand Grenade" and its upstairs bar "Top of the Trop" with a jukebox filled with Buffett's music; Woldenberg Park (1 Canal Place), noted in the "big gray rocks" he mentions in his song "The Shelter;" Hotel Villa Convento (616 Ursuline Avenue), where Buffett once lived (now room 305); and, of course, Buffett's defunct club and restaurant Margaritaville (1104 Decatur Street), where you can still see the sign positioned on the balcony. Buffett fans can still find a paradise of iconic tributes to the man affectionately known as Bubba and whose last words appropriately were "Have fun."

Address Miltenberger House, 900–910 Royal Street, New Orleans, LA 70116 | Hours Viewable 24 hours | Tip The Royal Street Pedestrian Mall is one of the best places to see buskers, particularly the 600 to 900 blocks of Royal Street.

80 Piazza d'Italia

Bright slice of Italy

In the late 19th and early 20th century, New Orleans welcomed tens of thousands of Italian immigrants, particularly Sicilians, making it second only to New York for Sicilian immigrants. For generations, the Italians' influence on New Orleans culture went largely unacknowledged, often overshadowed by French and Spanish influence.

In the 1970s, leaders from the Italian-American community conceived of a permanent public commemoration to honor their contributions to the city. To revitalize and redevelop the waterfront, a city block at the edge of the French Quarter and three blocks from the Mississippi River was chosen. The space was designed by noted postmodern architects Charles Moore and Perez Architects of New Orleans and completed in 1978. Initially, it was hailed as a postmodern masterpiece.

Intended as a "surprise plaza," it is an open circular area with rows of columns giving the illusion of an ancient Roman forum with its porticos and triumphal arches. There are references to Italian culture throughout the space, including an inlaid map of Italy in the pavement, modern versions of flying buttresses, white and olive stonework to represent medieval buildings, and a raised rostrum (speaker's platform). The Piazza's fountain is inscribed in Latin and split into two sections. On the left it reads *Fons Sancti Josephi* (The Fountain of Saint Joseph), and on the right, *Hvnc Fontem Cives Novi Avreliani Toto Populo Dono Dederunt* (The Citizens of New Orleans Have Given This Fountain to All the People as a Gift). But the bright colors, use of steel, and neon lights give it a quality that has been described as being "too Disney" and "cartoonish." Moore insisted it was a joyful tribute to Italians, even inserting himself in the space. His face spews water from his pursed smiling mouth on the arcs of the plaza. After years of neglect, it was restored in 2004, and regardless of its being hailed as a triumph to postmodernism or a kitschy disappointment, Moore achieved his ultimate goal – surprise.

Address 377 Poydras Street, New Orleans, LA 70130 | Hours Daily 7am–7pm | Tip The American Italian Cultural Center is part museum and part event space, and even offers classes in Italian.

81 Piety & Desire Chocolate

Chocolate lovers' crusade

The history of chocolate is one of discipline and desire. In civilizations around the world, the cacao bean has been used for sacred and secular purposes, as well as religious ceremonies and currency. This was not lost on New Orleans native Christopher Nobles who had a life-long interest in the humanities and science. For Nobles, who loved to cook but didn't enjoy the restaurant lifestyle, chocolate was the perfect convergence of both. And the name of his business, Piety & Desire Chocolate (based on beloved New Orleans street names), was the consummate reflection of his love for his city, expression for his passions, and the emotions chocolate stirs in others – the yearning and devotion in this luscious creation.

Most chocolatiers either manufacture their own chocolate or make their own confection. Nobles does both, which puts him in rarefied company in the chocolate industry and perfectly illustrates his shop's motto – "From Bean to Bar to Bon Bon and Beyond." Resembling exquisite jewels, the bon bons, both regular and seasonal, are the show-stealers. It is the "beyond," however, that distinguishes Nobles' desserts from others.

Nobles serves up Cajun drinking chocolate, a proprietary spice blend made in-house with traces of cayenne, smoked paprika, and thyme, as well as classic European sipping chocolate. The affogato, an Italian dessert made with a scoop of ice cream and espresso, and their chocolate bars – infused with local strawberries and pralines – also go beyond. Vegan options are available.

All of this can be enjoyed at Piety & Desire Chocolate, a former bar and po'boy shop from the 1930s, on historic Magazine Street surrounded by dozens of local shops. You are immediately transported to another place, surrounded by prints and paintings starring chocolate, over a 100-year-old, 25-foot mahogany bar that you can slide up to and order from, or tuck a box of bonbons and a couple bars into your bag and take the experience home with you.

Address 2032 Magazine Street, New Orleans, LA 70130 | Hours Mon & Tue, Thu–Sat 11am–6pm | Tip The chocolatier collaborates with Parleaux Beer Lab, a pet-friendly neighborhood beer garden and taproom in the Bywater.

82 Podesta's Bunny-Men

Bunnies on watch

If you are walking on Oretha Haley Castle Boulevard in Central City and you feel like someone is watching you, you are probably correct. Perched along a rooftop are five large bunny-man sculptures gazing down at you. These are the work of local artist Alex Podesta.

Born in North Carolina, he grew up in Virginia on an abandoned chicken farm to artist parents; Podesta's formal education comes from the Governor's Magnet School for the Arts in Virginia, Virginia Commonwealth, and the University of New Orleans. His early work was, according to Podesta, very cerebral and polished. As an artist, he felt he was playing it too safe and needed to take more risks. For Podesta, his greatest fear was inventing something that was too abjectly personal, so he decided to "rip the Band-aid off" and create a self-portraiture.

As a child, Podesta had a yellow onesie pajama set with white vinyl feet. Because Bugs Bunny had white feet, he felt like his pajamas were his own bunny suit. His first piece based on this theme was *Self-Portrait as Bunnies* in 2005 which featured two large sculptures made from plaster molds of Podesta's own body parts dressed in a bunny suit. More pieces followed, exploring the themes of creativity and the naïveté of youth.

Podesta's rooftop statue is called *City Watch* and is a loose riff on Auguste Rodin's *Burghers of Calais* statue, which represents an event that occurred during the Hundred Years' War when six French leaders of Calais surrendered to the English to save the city. The statue was meant to be placed at ground level, rather than on a pedestal. Affected by the damage of Hurricane Katrina, Podesta inverted Rodin's meaning by creating five half-figure bunny-men designed to go behind a parapet and watch over those below. The statues are not only meant as symbols of protection, but also as an homage to the countless people who were stranded on their roofs during Katrina.

Address 1220 Oretha Castle Haley Boulevard, New Orleans, LA 70113 | **Hours** Accessible 24 hours | **Tip** To get up close to some of Podesta's statues, you can visit one of his bunny-men in the lobby of the Virgin Hotel (550 Baronne Street) and even pose next to it.

83 Pontalba Buildings

Buildings born from a gunshot

Two brick-row houses perpendicular to St. Louis Cathedral represent the resolution and inventiveness of one woman. Micaela Leonarda Antonia de Almonester Rojas y de la Ronde was born into a life of privilege in 1795. Her mother, a wealthy renowned French Creole beauty, married Don Andres Almonester y Rojas in 1787. Almonester was an affluent Spanish civil servant and philanthropist 30 years her senior who helped fund the construction of St. Louis Cathedral, The Presbytère, and The Cabildo. When Micaela was two and a half, Don died, and she inherited a fortune; when she was 15, a marriage was arranged for her – to her 20-year-old cousin Joseph-Xavier Célestin Delfau de Pontalba. The marriage, which was regarded as a business merger, quickly became a hostile takeover. Micaela's father-in-law, the Baron, repeatedly tried to get Micaela to turn over her estate to him using threats, coercion, and emotional abuse. In 1834, frustrated over her refusals, he shot Micaela in the chest four times at point-blank range with a pair of dueling pistols. Micaela's left breast and two fingers were mutilated, but she survived. The Baron killed himself on the very night of the attack with his own dueling pistols. His death gave Micaela her own inheritance – the title of Baroness Pontalba.

The Baroness returned to New Orleans in 1848, with a slight disfigurement and a new determination. She tore down the existing buildings facing Jackson Square and replaced them with matching red-brick, four-story buildings that are today known as the Pontalba Buildings. These cast-iron galleries are thought to be the first in New Orleans, and they became the fashion of the day. The Baroness left New Orleans in 1851 and died in Paris in 1874. The iconic buildings are now used as shops and apartments, but the Baroness' mark is still apparent. Look closely and you will find her monogram AP (Almonester and Pontalba) gracefully woven in the ironwork, a testament to her style and her iron will.

Address Jackson Square, 500 blocks of St. Ann and St. Peter Streets, New Orleans, LA 70116 | **Hours** Viewable from the outside only | **Tip** The 1850 House located in the building is a museum furnished with the art and décor of a prosperous mid 19th-century family in New Orleans. It has a lovely gift shop.

84 Prayer Window

Vision of sainthood

St. Louis Cathedral in Jackson Square is the oldest continuously operating cathedral in the country. It is also one of the few Roman Catholic churches that is located on a large public square, making it an ideal location for both the religious and revelers to converge. Inside, worshippers pursue prayer and penance, while outside, visitors and street performers pursue pleasure and profit. While the cathedral is an instantly recognizable and lionized building in the city, inside a prayer room are two stained glass windows dedicated to a lesser-known religious figure. Created by artist Ruth Goliwas in 2008, the windows depict New Orleans native Henriette DeLille.

Born in 1812, the fourth generation of free people of color, DeLille was light-skinned enough to pass as white (her parents and siblings registered as white), but DeLille refused, which limited her opportunities. After the death of her two children born out of wedlock, the 24-year-old DeLille experienced a religious transformation and formed the Sisters of the Holy Family Order in 1842, a Catholic religious order of African American nuns who nursed the sick and taught people of color. She died in 1862.

The Catholic Church, acknowledging DeLille's impact, declared her a Servant of God in 2010, the first step in the formal process of canonization. The next step is the approval of two miracles attributed to the prayer-prompted intercession by DeLille. The church is currently reviewing those miracles and, if approved, DeLille will be declared a saint in New Orleans, the first who wasn't donning a uniform and holding a football.

The prayer room, located in the former baptistery, features one window of DeLille holding an infant and another full-length one of her with small children and an elderly woman, representing all the benevolence she showed to the disadvantaged and impoverished in New Orleans.

Address 615 Pere Antoine Alley, New Orleans, LA 70116 | Hours Daily 9am–4pm | Tip Behind the cathedral on Royal Street there is also a commemorative plaque dedicated to Henriette DeLille.

85 Pulcinella!

A delicious intersection

As a trained ballerina, burlesque dancer Bella Blue perfected the pirouette, but the most important move she has learned is how to pivot. In 2020, Blue was set to embark on a tour that started in San Francisco and ended in South Korea. One of her performances was an homage to Pierrot the clown, a character from Italy's 17th-century Commedia dell'arte that she has adored since childhood. When the tour was cancelled because of Covid, Blue remained in New Orleans, met her future husband Andrew Principe, and together they opened a business that combined Principe's love of food and Blue's love of performing and teaching. They found the perfect two-story venue in the 7th Ward with a grandfathered-in 24/7 license. The upstairs was the original Nite Cap, owned by Alfred Doucette, and was considered by many to be the birthplace of funk in New Orleans, hosting bands such as the Meters and the Batiste Brothers. To honor Doucette's legacy, they kept the name. The restaurant was named Pulcinella after another clown from the Commedia dell'arte and to honor Principe's Sicilian roots.

Pulcinella, which is becoming rapidly known for its savory fare and thoughtful wine list, is an intimate place decorated in warm jewel colors with Principe's family photos and Blue's collection of clowns. Blue believes the skills she learned working in a strip club, running a Victoria's Secret store, producing burlesque shows, and being a mom, have all led her to become the restaurant's Headmistress of Hospitality. "It's easy to earn trust with good food," she says, "but the linchpin is to make them feel welcome." Bella, who does double duty greeting people and bringing food to patrons in Pulcinella downstairs, brings that same attitude to Nite Cap upstairs. Bella's Whiskey & Rhinestones is the house show, and there are multiple other acts, including choirs, comedy nights, and the popular "Stripparaoke," which combines stripping and karaoke.

It's important to Principe and Blue that both spaces are inclusive, but as always, for the chameleon Blue, her pivots often come with a touch of bump and grind.

Address Pulcinella!, 1300 St. Bernard Avenue, First Floor, New Orleans, LA 70116; Nite Cap located on second floor | Hours Pulcinella! Thu–Mon 5:30–9:30pm, Nite Cap Thu–Mon 6pm–late | Tip Kermit's Treme Mother-in-Law Lounge is a few blocks away and owned by musician Kermit Ruffins. It's a lively music venue and bar, and Ruffins frequently hosts cookouts in the back patio.

86 Rebirth Statue

No white flags

Emotions were high during the New Orleans Saints football team's return to the Superdome on September 25, 2006. It was the first time New Orleans had hosted an NFL game after the devastation of Hurricane Katrina. The game was also a division game against their archrival Atlanta Falcons. Regarded as the "Domecoming," it was the biggest regular-season game in Saints history. There were 75,000 people in the stadium, as well as thousands more outside watching as Saints safety Steve Gleason blocked the ball off the foot of then-Atlanta punter Michael Koenen and into the end zone for a Saints touchdown in the first quarter of the game. The roar from the crowd was deafening. The Saints would go on to beat the Falcons 24-3. *Times-Picayune* photographer Michael DeMocker took a photo of Gleason's outstretched hands as he dove toward the football. Years later, those who witnessed it still speak about the energy and electricity that vibrated through the city as a triumph after a year of unspeakable tragedy.

Plans were made to commemorate the event. Nationally acclaimed New Jersey sculptor Brian Hanlon was chosen to immortalize the moment, which ultimately became the de facto symbol of the city's resilience. Standing at almost nine feet tall, the bronze statue entitled *Rebirth* shows the instant when Gleason blocked the punt. It was unveiled in 2012 and took on even more heroic proportions as Gleason had been diagnosed in 2011 with ALS (amyotrophic lateral sclerosis), also known as Lou Gehrig's disease. The man who hurled himself in front of the football was now in a motorized wheelchair. That same year, Gleason started the nonprofit Team Gleason, which assists people with ALS. Of the statue, Gleason said, "But I just don't want this to be about me and that play. I want it to be about what the play symbolized, which was a commitment by this community to rebuild. This statue is about coming through adversity. It's about finding your heroes. It's about commitment and a rebirth for all."

Address Caesars Superdome, 1500 Sugar Bowl Drive, New Orleans, LA 70112 | Hours Viewable 24 hours | Tip "No White Flags" is Gleason's mantra and means to keep fighting and not give up in the face of challenges. It is also the mantra for his charity, Team Gleason, which works to improve the lives of people living with ALS (www.teamgleason.org).

87 Ricca's Architectural Sales

Salvaged delight

It's common to find multi-generational businesses in New Orleans, but in the antique business, it can't be lost on the employees of Ricca's Architectural Sales that modern items that were available when Peter Ricca started the business in 1956 are now considered antiques. With three warehouses, a mill shop, and a brickyard, it is easy to get overwhelmed. When asking for help, however, it's not uncommon to hear the reply, "Let me ask my cousin/brother/aunt." Ricca's is a family business in the truest sense, in its ancestry and in its employees. Many of the workers have been with the business since the current owners and managers were in grade school.

The main warehouse is housed in a former space to build lifeboats and life jackets for LCVPs (landing craft, vehicle, personnel) known as Higgins Boats (after Andrew Higgins the businessman and founder of the boats) used in World War II by the Allied forces in amphibious landings. Today, the area is filled with Victorian and craftsman-made stained glass windows, Art Deco doorknobs, Murano and Art Nouveau pendant chandeliers, Tiffany lamps, metal gas station signs, Eastlake-style carved walnut brackets, wood face corbels, old glass Coca-Cola bottles, and cast-iron fireplace covers.

Reclaimed lumber, however, is their main attraction. Rows and rows of doors of every style, size, and type of wood line the aisles, along with windows, shutters, mantels, and shelves. Most of them are salvaged from old houses all over the Gulf South while others are new and custom-made. The outdoor area has everything from antique cast-iron benches, giant plaster lions, steel hitching posts, and wrought-iron gates with rosettes. Every corner of the business is an opportunity for discovery, and an entire afternoon can be spent wandering the warehouses listening to the music of a local radio station in the background. The saying "What's old is new again" couldn't be truer for this multi-generational business, but in their case, it is true "again and again."

Address 511 N. Solomon Street, New Orleans, LA 70119 | Hours Tue–Fri 9am–4pm, Sat 9am–2pm | Tip In the theme of family-run businesses, Clesi's Seafood Restaurant located nearby is an award-winning family-run restaurant that specializes in boiled local crawfish and classic New Orleans dishes.

88 Roosevelt Clock

Watching the history of time

In today's world, where the time of day is flashing in neon from every direction or even notifies you by gentle vibrations on your wrist, it's refreshing to stop and watch time pass.

The Roosevelt Hotel is the quintessential blend of history and modernity. It is known for its landmark bar, the Sazerac Bar, its elaborate and superlative Christmas decorations, and for hosting one of the United States' first modern nightclubs (The Cave). It was corrupt Louisiana Governor Huey P. Long's favorite place to lounge in his silk pajamas from his 12th-floor suite, sipping his Ramos Gin Fizz, and giving orders to his cronies. However, it is lesser known for its exquisite antiques.

Originally built as the Grunewald Hotel in 1893, it came under new ownership and was rebranded the Roosevelt Hotel in 1923 after the indomitable spirit of former President Teddy Roosevelt. The hotel suffered extensive damage from Hurricane Katrina and was eventually purchased and restored under the exclusive Waldorf Astoria Collection brand. Following the Waldorf Astoria's tradition of having a stately signature clock in each of its hotels, the company purchased the 19th-century clock known as the Paris Exhibition Clock, appropriately named since it was featured in the Paris Exhibition of 1867. Crafted by French artisans Eugène Farcot and Albert-Ernest Carrier-Belleuse, this timepiece stands at the entrance on Roosevelt Way, is almost 10 feet tall, and is the largest conical clock known to exist, meaning the pendulum moves in a circular motion instead of side to side as in a regular clock. Situated below the clock dial is a bronze inlay of the cherub Chronos, who in Greek mythology is the god of time. The face of the clock is laid out with Roman numerals and diamond-shaped minute markers with moon-shaped hands. The base is carved from Algerian onyx and atop it is a gilt-bronze sculpture of a woman in classical dress holding a scepter that rotates soundlessly and constantly, keeping the time and adding to the majesty and mystery.

Address The Roosevelt Hotel, 130 Roosevelt Way, New Orleans, LA 70112 | Tip The historic Orpheum Theater is right across the street and offers everything from ballet, burlesque, symphonies, and traveling comedy acts.

89 Rosalie Alley

Hidden vodou

What exists between piety and desire is a debate for the ages. But what lies between Piety and Desire Streets in the Bywater is certain. This inconspicuous tree-shaded alley is, at first glance, easy to miss but it is a union of culture, art, and religion.

As legend has it, the alley's name comes from a "local character" in the early 20th century who once lived in the neighborhood, but it has now become a popular spot for Vodou rituals. The alley, which backs up to various homes, has a wooden fence painted with various Vodou symbols, including two intertwined snakes, which in Vodou represents the duality of forces, symbolizing the positive and negative aspects of life. There is also a variety of hearts, including a traditional Catholic sacred heart as well as one depicting Erzulie Dantor, the Vodou goddess of love, romance, and sex. The best way to describe some of the other paintings is "humorous macabre." Skulls are the dominant symbol, be they traditional or wearing a tuxedo and top hat and smoking a cigarette or dancing merrily. One such skull wears an eye patch reminiscent of the one that jazz piano player James Booker wore. Others are mermaid skeletons.

La Source Ancienne Ounfo, a private Vodou society whose mission is to create a lifestyle of growth, support, and service to the Lwa (the primary spirits of Vodous) frequently hold events here.

Vodou arrived in New Orleans with enslaved West Africans, who melded their religious rituals and practices with those of local Catholics. The Haitian Revolution (1791–1804) led to a mass exodus of refugees, including white colonists, free people of color, and the enslaved, doubling the population in one year. It also strengthened and increased the Vodou religion, which influenced the city's culture, food, music, and religious traditions. While many Vodou practitioners are also baptized Catholics, the sentiment of acceptance does not seem to be reciprocal. On the tomb of the famous Vodou priestess Marie Laveau it reads that she was involved in the "mystical cult 'voodooism.'"

Address 3319 Rosalie Alley, New Orleans, LA 70117 | Tip Pizza Delicious is nearby, started by two New Yorkers who loved New Orleans but missed authentic New York pizza.

90 The St. Charles Streetcar

A ride to the movie set

The St. Charles Streetcar line, running since 1835, is the oldest continuously operating streetcar line in the world. It's also the perfect opportunity for eagle-eyed fans of the big and small screen to see where some of their favorite movies and television shows have been filmed along the route.

Gallier Hall (545 St. Charles Avenue): Built by James Gallier, it is considered one of the finest examples of Greek Revival architecture in the country. It can also be seen in *Miller's Crossing, Runaway Jury,* and *Interview with the Vampire* (TV series).

Pontchartrain Hotel (2031 St. Charles Avenue): Dr. Rowan Fielding from the TV series *Mayfair Witches* stays at this opulent hotel.

The Columns Hotel (3811 St. Charles Avenue): Built in 1883 as a private residence and has one of the best places on the avenue to sit on the front porch and enjoy a cocktail while you watch the streetcar pass. *Pretty Baby* and *12 Years a Slave* were filmed there.

W. P. Brown House (4717 St. Charles Avenue): This Romanesque Revival mansion was built in 1904 and makes an appearance in *Green Book,* and the TV series *The Purge* and *Preacher.*

If you get off the streetcar and walk around the campuses of Tulane (6823 St. Charles Avenue) and Loyola (6363 St. Charles Avenue) Universities, you will find multiple film and TV locations from *22 Jump Street, Bad Moms, Jurassic World, The Big Short, Our Brand is Crisis, Happy Death Day, NCIS: New Orleans* and *Scream Queens.*

Toward the end of the avenue, you will find 7904 St. Charles Avenue, which was the "Barton Arms" apartments in *Miller's Crossing.*

Around the bend is the landmark diner The Camellia Grill (626 S. Carrollton Avenue) which served actors in *Green Book* and *American Horror Story* (TV series).

The iconic streetcar itself has appeared in multiple movies and TV shows, including *Angel Heart, Runaway Jury, The Pelican Brief, Your Honor* (TV) and, of course, *A Streetcar Named Desire.*

Address Route 12 of the St. Charles Streetcar line starts at Canal and Carondelet and ends at S. Carrollton and S. Claiborne Avenues | Hours Daily 24 hours (more frequent 7am–10pm, less frequent 10pm–6am) | Tip We can credit one of our most famous sandwiches to the 1929 streetcar strike. Martin Brothers' Coffee Stand and Restaurant gave the workers free baguette sandwiches during the strike. Allegedly, any time one of the workers entered their restaurant, the owners shouted, "Here comes another poor boy!" New Orleans' first "po-boys" were born.

91 Saint Expedite

Better than FedEx

When yellow fever ravaged New Orleans in the early 19th century, parishioners built the Chapel of St. Anthony of Padua (aka the Mortuary Chapel) in 1826 to serve as a burial church for yellow fever victims. Built near St. Louis Cemetery No. 1 and No. 2, it is the oldest surviving church in the city, having never needed to be rebuilt to the extent of others, like St. Louis Cathedral. It was renamed Our Lady of Guadalupe Chapel in 1918, right around the time a beloved local fable was created.

As legend goes, around 1921, the nuns of the church received a crate. Inside was a statue of an unidentified helmetless Roman soldier. In his left hand, instead of a sword, he held a palm branch close to his chest, symbolizing victory, martyrdom, and the triumph of humility over pride. In his raised right hand, he held a cross with the word *hodie* (Latin for "today") on it. There was no note inside, but the outside of the crate was marked "expedite," which may (or may not) have meant that it was a rush order. Regardless, the statue was placed near the right-hand corner of the entrance to the church, named St. Expedite; for generations, it has been inspiring prayers to him for those seeking quick resolutions. Vodou practitioners have also taken a liking to St. Expedite and have added him to their religion.

The church is also known for being the International Shrine of St. Jude, the patron saint of hope and lost causes, and for serving as the official chapel of the city's police and fire departments. Just outside of the church is a grotto built in honor of Our Lady of Lourdes, a title of the Virgin Mary.

While Our Lady of Guadalupe Chapel offers a variety of saints to choose from, St. Expedite is the only one with the hope of a speedy solution. According to local tradition, when St. Expedite intercedes on your behalf, it is customary to leave him a pound cake as thanks. Rumor has it that Sara Lee's pound cake is his favorite.

Address 411 N. Rampart Street, New Orleans, LA 70112 | Hours Mon–Sat 6am–11pm, Sun 7am–8pm | Tip The Saint Joan of Arc statue located in a small park near the French Market is a gift from France. Locals affectionately call it "Joanie on the Pony."

92 Scrap House

A Hurricane Katrina memorial

Located upriver from Canal Street on the banks of the Mississippi River is the Ernest N. Morial Convention Center, one of the largest convention centers in the country, which covers 11 blocks and over 3 million square feet of space. It is frequently ranked in the top 10 for meeting venues and is renowned for its sleek, progressive, and green-friendly design. Its 7.5-acre Pedestrian Park features large public artworks polished to a sheen to represent the Mississippi River, Meditation, and Music. But directly across the street is the Mississippi River Heritage Park, a modest 1.36-acre park with typical green space of trees and benches. At the park's entrance is a unique folk-art piece in stark contrast to the chic modernity that dominates much of the area.

The *Scrap House* sculpture, created by local artist Sally Heller, is a recognition of the fortitude of the people of New Orleans following Hurricane Katrina. The work, made possible from a grant from the Joan Mitchell Center, was only supposed to be on display for two years, but its emotional impact resonated with the people, and the piece has remained. Heller, who said she has always been fascinated with "the way we talk with imagery," used salvaged pieces to depict a classic shotgun-style house lodged in a tree. After Hurricane Katrina, the artist was jolted by the "bizarre hybrids" and discordance of seeing boats balancing on trees, overturned cars stacked on top of each other, and iconic restaurant and store signs laying askew in the middle of the street.

Heller purchased 55-gallon oil drums off Craigslist and worked with artist Travis Linde to fabricate the trunk and bark of the tree. The house itself is made from distressed salvage cypress wood, and because of this, it had to eventually be refurbished. The sculpture flawlessly recreates a surreal image of what for many was a reality, and represents the endurance of New Orleans' spirit in the face of tragedy.

Address 1201 Convention Center Boulevard, New Orleans, LA 70130 | Tip The Louisiana Civil Rights Museum is on Convention Center Boulevard; opened in 2021, it allows visitors to experience the movement through archival videos and firsthand oral histories.

93 Seasons in the Square

Climate change

With New Orleans' humid subtropical climate, it is a common joke that the city's seasons don't correlate with the weather. In New Orleans, the seasons are Mardi Gras Season (Winter), Festival Season (Spring), Hurricane Season (Summer), and Football Season (Fall). But most do not know that all the typical seasons are represented in Jackson Square Park, and they are believed to be the city' oldest existing statues.

Originally designed as a military parade ground and called *Place d'Armes* during the French colonial period and then *Plaza de Armas* during Spanish rule, this 2.5-acre public square was renamed Jackson Square in 1851 to honor General Andrew Jackson's victory over the British at the Battle of New Orleans. Five years later, approximately 60,000 individuals crowded the square for the unveiling of Clark Mill's new sculpture. The 20,000-pound sculpture depicts Jackson on horseback as he reviewed his troops on the morning of January 8, 1815, before the battle. It is the centerpiece of the square and for almost 170 years has survived multiple hurricanes and storms that have battered the square. But lesser known are four statues that have been standing guard in the square for even longer.

At each corner of the square are four marble neoclassical statues representing the personifications of the four seasons. They date back to 1851. On January 17, 1852 a newspaper article stated that the statues were received from the North months earlier and are "very chaste and elegant monuments." Information on the artist is not listed. *Spring*, located in the southwest corner, is represented as a young woman holding a bouquet in one hand and a wreath in the other; *Summer*, located in the northeast corner, is characterized as a young man leaning against a tree with a book in one hand and grapes in the other; *Autumn*, located in the southeast corner, is portrayed by an older woman holding a scythe; *Winter*, located in the northwest corner, is depicted as an old, bearded man wrapped in a cloak. While New Orleans might not have traditional seasons, at least they have beautiful statues as reminders.

Address Bound by Chartres Street and St. Ann Street, Decatur Street and St. Peter Street | Hours Daily 8am–6pm (winter), 8am–7pm (daylight saving time) | Tip If you are a first timer eating a beignet at Café du Monde, it is good luck to have your eating partner blow powdered sugar on your face.

94_The Singing Oak

Chime tree

City Park is home to the largest collection of Live Oak trees in the world, but only one of them sings. Native to the southeastern coast, Live Oaks differ from regular oak trees as they don't lose all their leaves in the fall, instead losing and replacing all year, thus remaining "live" year-round. Some of the Live Oaks in the park are over 800 years old. With their curved trunks and meandering branches that spread in all directions, one tree located just east of the Big Lake in City Park stands out: the Singing Oak.

Still considered a youngster among the other trees at approximately 100 years old, the Singing Oak is known for the large-scale chimes hanging from its serpentine branches. Local artist Jim Hart, who spent his childhood summers playing in City Park, wanted to give back after Hurricane Katrina, when roughly 2,000 of its Live Oaks were destroyed from the massive flooding and levee failures. Typically, Live Oaks can withstand high winds due to their immense trunks and remarkable root system. Since Hurricane Katrina, City Park has replanted over 6,400 trees of different species.

Although the visual landscape of City Park at the Singing Oak's location conjures feelings of serenity and balance between its wildlife, wetlands, jogging paths, and various art installations, the area was still plagued by the noise generated by busy Wisner Avenue, which runs parallel to the park.

Hart strung up a set of aluminum alloy tubes of different sizes using the same pentatonic scale (five notes per octave) employed in West African music, old hymnals, and early New Orleans jazz. Hart noted that early jazz was (and still is) improvisational, and nothing was more improvisational than the wind.

Locals and tourists gather underneath the tree for outdoor naps, meditation, picnics, or yoga. Adding to the ambience, an auspicious plaque beneath the tree reads: *Let the wind bring you a melody, a smile, and a sense of peace and nature.*

Address City Park, One Palm Drive, New Orleans, LA 70124 | Tip After a moment of Zen, visit another famous oak, the Dueling Oak, where Creoles would slash each other over hints at the slightest improprieties.

95 Skelly Tomb

A miniature medieval castle

The historic St. Louis Cemetery No. 3 is the largest – at 19 acres – and the best maintained of the Catholic cemeteries in New Orleans. It's home to centuries-old tombs with angels perched above and intricately carved flowers, crosses, and other symbols on its tablets.

One tomb, however, is the antithesis to all the others. The Skelly Tomb is a large gray granite mausoleum in the design of a medieval castle. The imposing structure was built by Alfortish Enterprises and features Gothic-style windows with stained glass and bronze doors and window frames. It's a popular spot for tours, where guides spin tales about how Skelly built this tomb out of spite to keep her greedy daughters from getting her inheritance, and then forbid them to be buried with her. None of this, however, is true.

Born in 1925, Beverly Skelly was married six times and had two sons by different husbands. Her first son, even though he had predeceased her by seven years, was still disinherited for good measure. According to Blake Alfortish, Skelly wanted a tomb modeled after old French castles, complete with turrets and statues of archers on top. She got the turrets but not the archers. Skelly also wanted to have her two dogs, a part Irish Wolfhound, part Doberman named Tim Leary, and a Pekingese named Max, which she had stuffed years before, dipped in gold and placed outside her tomb. The Catholic Church denied her request. It was allowed to have statues of your dogs, just not have your dogs as statues.

How Skelly got the money to buy the plot and build the tomb in 2011 at the cost of approximately $600,000 is still a mystery. But what isn't are the new owners. Skelly died in 2017 at the age of 91 and left her tomb to the SPCA, the Society for the Protection of Cruelty Against Animals. The nonprofit now owns the spacious mausoleum with one woman in it. What happened to Tim Leary and Max is also a mystery, but the castle tomb represents another example of how truth is always stranger than fiction.

Address St. Louis Cemetery No. 3, 3421 Esplanade Avenue, New Orleans, LA 70119 | Hours Mon–Sat 8am–4:30pm, Sun & holidays 8am–4pm | Tip Across the street from St. Louis Cemetery No. 3 is Cabrini High School. The Grotto to Our Lady of Lourdes faces Esplanade Avenue. It was established in 1851 by a mother who was grateful for her son's return from World War II.

96 Sophia Loren Statue

Bronze Italian goddess

The first question one might ask when they find a brightly polished bronze surrealist statue of a woman nestled in a corner of the Botanical Gardens in City Park is, "Who is that?" Upon discovering it is Italian actress Sophia Loren, the next question might be, "Why?"

The sculpture is the work of the successful and contemporary Italian filmmaker and artist Francesco Vezzoli, whose work is often described as depicting strong allegories about modern culture. His art has been shown around the world in such venues as the Tate Modern in London, Solomon R. Guggenheim Museum and The Metropolitan Museum of Art in New York, The Museum of Contemporary Art in Los Angeles, Grand Palais in Paris, and the Nouveau Musée National de Monaco, among others.

The 75-inch by 23-inch by 23-inch sculpture features Loren as the Muse of Antiquity. While many can recognize Loren's facial features, the statue does not pay homage to her famous curvaceous figure; instead it represents her with a slender, svelte figure. Loren is clutching a pile of classical pillars, arches and pediments to her chest. This visual was inspired by World War I-era paintings from Italian artist and writer Giorgio de Chirico, who founded the *scuola metafisica* art movement, which had a profound influence on the surrealists.

The sculpture was a part of Prospect New Orleans, an organization founded after Hurricane Katrina to invite artists from all over the globe to create pieces in venues throughout New Orleans. Their goal was to "bring new art to an old city." The project has continued and occurs every three years. Many of the projects are influenced by social justice issues and the city of New Orleans itself. Vezzoli's Sophia Loren statue was part of Prospect 2 in 2011 and was initially housed in the Piazza d'Italia. It was later moved to a corner of the 10 acres of the Botanical Garden in City Park. The bronzed Muse of Antiquity is perfectly at home with the vibrant flora of the city.

Address Botanical Garden, City Park, 5 Victory Avenue, New Orleans, LA 70124 | Hours Tue–Sun 10am–4:30pm | Tip The Botanical Garden has over 2,000 varieties of plants from around the world. The Enrique Alférez Sculpture Garden showcases the work of the artist and houses 15 of his sculptures surrounded by oak trees and greenery.

97 Spirit House

Listening to the spirits

Gentilly, known as the "long neighborhood," is built on a naturally occurring ridge and runs by Lake Pontchartrain to the north and Bayou St. John to the west. It is known architecturally for its shotguns, bungalows, and ranch-style houses, as well as wide lawns, off-street parking, and graceful old oak trees. Seen more as a typical suburb, it is one of the city's largest and most racially diverse neighborhoods. It suffered extensive damage during Hurricane Katrina and has been slowly rebuilding. A sculpture by local artists captures the historical and modern-day spirit of New Orleans, as well as the neighborhood it is located in.

Centrally located at De Saix Circle, artists John T. Scott and Martin Payton produced a striking 19-foot aluminum structure that simultaneously conjures both a majestic cathedral and a simple shotgun house. Called *Spirit House*, the piece was commissioned by the Percent for Art Program of the City of New Orleans. Scott, a nationally known artist and fine-art professor at Xavier University for over 40 years, collaborated with one of his former students Martin Payton in building the piece. Scott's goal was to create a sculpture that celebrated the cultural and physical contributions of African Americans in New Orleans. The silhouetted figures of the cut-out sculpture represent drawings from the artists and local schoolchildren, as well as varying cultural and religious iconography: a Chi Wara antelope head from the Bamana people of Mali, ancient Egyptian hieroglyphs, and a crucifix. More modern symbols include silhouettes of jazz musicians, laborers, church choirs, animals, and poetic inscriptions. The brilliance is that each angle tells a story like each room in a house or chapter in a book.

Scott is quoted as saying, "New Orleans is the only city that I've been in that if you listen to the sidewalks, they will speak to you." In this case, if you stand under the *Spirit House* and listen, perhaps the spirits will speak to you.

Address A median in Gentilly between St. Bernard Avenue and De Saix Boulevard | Tip *Spirit Gates,* located on the right side of the New Orleans Museum of Art, which was built as a testament to Black artists in New Orleans, was also built by John T. Scott.

98 St. Ann Shrine

A miracle in matrimony

Located near houses, apartment buildings, and even a barbershop, in the Treme neighborhood, is a replica of the grotto in Lourdes, France where Roman Catholics believe the Virgin Mary appeared in 1858. In the Catholic tradition, St. Ann is venerated as Mary's mother. Dedicated on July 26, 1902, the feast day of Saint Ann, the grotto was originally maintained by the church, but for the last few decades, it has been maintained by volunteer caretakers.

Once you enter the grotto, a version of Rome's "Scala Sancta," or Holy Stairs, is located on the right. To ascend the "Stations of the Cross" stairway, you must kneel and crawl up the stairs. It is customary to pray the way of the cross along the way as you view weathered bas-relief sculptures depicting the stations of the cross hanging on the walls. Many pray for healing, protection, or the granting of miracles, but for decades, the miracle many women sought here was the miracle of matrimony. It was customary for women in search of a husband to crawl up the stairs praying silently or aloud, "St. Ann, St. Ann, give me a man."

If your devotion (or knees) are not up to the challenge, you can walk up the left side of the stairs. At the top of the open-air space is a 15-foot statue of Jesus hanging on the cross with Mary and John the Baptist standing on either side and Mary Magdalene kneeling in the center. The statue is dedicated to the memory of deceased family members of restaurater Edgar Dooky L. Chase.

The grounds of this corner lot contain several other religious statues, including a small image of Saint Joseph, where people leave keys in hopes for assistance in finding housing.

A New Orleans Good Friday tradition for many Catholics is the "Making of Nine Churches." This involves making a special devotion by walking to nine churches to pray. The shrine, not officially a church, however, counts as one, making it the only stop where both housing and husbands are sought by the parishioners.

Address 2101 Ursuline Avenue, New Orleans, LA 70116 | Hours Tue, Thu & Sat 9am–noon | Tip If you are hungry after climbing the stairs, Li'l Dizzy's Café, owned for decades by the Baquet family, serves Creole Soul food and is said to have the best fried chicken in the city (1500 Esplanade Avenue).

99 STELLA!

Tennessee Williams' dwellings

Playwright Tennessee Williams once famously said, "America has only three cities: New York, San Francisco, and New Orleans. Everywhere else is Cleveland." And Williams' favorite New Orleans neighborhood in his self-proclaimed "spiritual home" was the French Quarter.

Williams first arrived in the French Quarter in 1938. In a 1974 interview with Dick Cavett, Williams said he was first shocked by the "bohemianess" of the quarter, but it had since become his "natural ambiance." Williams lived in apartments and houses on and off in the quarter for the rest of his life, but three of them stand out.

One of the first places Williams called home was 722 Toulouse Street in an attic apartment. It was there he wrote his short story "The Angel in the Alcove." He also experimented with different pen names, including Valentine Xavier, but after believing it sounded too pompous, Thomas Williams decided on Tennessee. This apartment served as the setting for his 1970s play *Vieux Carré* and is now owned by the Historic New Orleans Collection.

At 632½ St. Peter Street, Williams wrote at least half of his Pulitzer-prize-winning play *A Streetcar Named Desire*, completing it in 1947. Although he only lived at this apartment a short time, it was crucial for Williams' inspiration as he could hear the streetcar as he wrote. This apartment is most associated with Williams' play and sometimes people walk by and holler up, "STELLLA!"

The first home Williams owned was 1014 Dumaine Street. He purchased the 1835 Greek Revival building in 1962. It had three full-floor apartments and three small ones in two dependencies. Williams lived in the second-floor apartment B on and off until his death in 1983. In his 1975 autobiography, Williams hoped he would die in his sleep in his big brass bed in this apartment. Sadly, he passed away in New York.

If you feel awkward yelling "STELLLA!" by yourself, don't fret. Every spring the Tennessee Williams Festival holds the Stella Shouting Contest, where hundreds gather and scream their angst into the world.

Hours Viewable from the outside only | Tip The balcony from which Elvis sings "Crawfish" in the opening of the movie *King Creole* is located on the second-floor gallery at 1018 Royal Street.

100 Storyland

Climb Jack's beanstalk

Opened a few days after Christmas in 1956, Storyland in City Park has been an institution for generations. Surrounded by immense oaks swathed with Spanish moss, children can climb, crawl, and slide over larger-than-life iconic characters from classic fairy tales. Originally, Storyland contained live animals, including chickens, rabbits, pigs, a lamb and two geese. But over time, some of the animals never appeared to age. A woman called asking if it was possible for lambs to suffer from schizophrenia because the once docile lamb was suddenly "hostile." The park's general manager Ellis Laborde revealed he made special arrangements with a St. Bernard Parish farmer to have the lamb and the three little pigs replaced every six weeks to keep the illusion of the nursery rhyme "Mary Had a Little Lamb" and the fairy tale "Three Little Pigs". Laborde said they could "preserve the illusion of eternal youth," and the breeder got his animals back a little bit fatter.

In 2019, the park had its first major makeover in 35 years, which merged the nostalgic charm with new ADA accessibility modifications and incorporated STEM and interactive exhibits. Now Captain Hook's pirate ship and the "Hey Diddle Diddle" exhibit are ADA accessible, with the latter teaching NASA's history. "Pinocchio and the Whale" used to be a place for children to climb in and pretend to be eaten, but now inside the space is a projected image of a school of fish that swim away when a child tries to catch them. And kids can read the Wolf's line from the "Three Little Pigs" from a device that transforms their voice into a low rumbling growl. But they have maintained their original vision – a new three-story "Jack and the Beanstalk" jungle gym with a covered tunnel slide is now available.

While live animals are no longer there to perpetuate the impression of eternal youth, Storyland still entertains and enchants the young and young at heart.

Address 5 Victory Avenue, New Orleans, LA 70124 | Hours Tue–Sun 10am–4:30pm | Tip The Sydney and Walda Besthoff Sculpture Garden is just a short walk away and features over 90 sculptures in a beautifully landscaped 12-acre site.

101 Storyville Museum

An excursion into New Orleans' red-light district

In the 1890s, overwhelmed with the brothels materializing all over New Orleans, alderman Sidney Story drafted an ordinance that made prostitution illegal everywhere in the city except for a section in the Treme neighborhood. Much to Story's dismay, he received the dubious honor of having the area nicknamed after him: Storyville. From 1897 until its closing in 1917, these 14 square blocks of sin offered hot jazz, cold drinks, and warm flesh for sale of all varieties and proclivities.

Over 100 years after the red lights dimmed, the district has been widely misrepresented. Enter New Orleans native Claus Sadlier. "It is a story that needed to be told in a beginning and end fashion," Sadlier states. Recognizing that Storyville wasn't limited to its salaciousness, Sadlier resolved to use Storyville as a substratum to talk about New Orleans' history and its significance in America's early development.

Completely self-funded, the museum leads visitors through the city's early days as a French colony, its influence as a port city, and its equal embrace of urbanity and iniquity. Some of the museum's most fascinating objects are the 1907 and 1914 *Blue Books*, literal guidebooks to Storyville and a reflection of the burgeoning consumer culture and transactional nature of pleasure. Visitors can view the pages containing the names of the prostitutes and their "work" address, ads for various upscale brothels, liquors (ranging from fine champagnes to modest beers), and even cures for venereal diseases. You can also view many of the actual products, from the contraceptives to the contraband. Local artists' murals depict brothels on Basin Street (the Rodeo Drive for prostitutes) that could cost a patron their entire paycheck, as well as the ramshackle "cribs" – where pleasures were often procured with pocket change. Listening stations play the earliest jazz record, an entire section is dedicated to E. J. Bellocq's stunning photographs of Storyville prostitutes, and there are even hologram portrayals of women of that era. Each corner of the over 7,000 square-foot space is an educational and visceral experience rooted in history and authenticity.

Address 1010 Conti Street, New Orleans, LA 70112 | **Hours** Daily 9am–6pm (over 18s only) | **Tip** A few blocks down, on Burgundy Street, look for a metal gate in front of a courtyard. There you should find Iko, a cockatoo, owned by Dr. John's former road manager, who for over 25 years has been saying "hello" to passersby.

102 Studio Be

Radical imagination

Brandan "BMIKE" Odums can't remember a time when he wasn't creating art. "It's always a language I spoke," he says, and through his life, he was challenged to speak art in many ways. Studio Be, a 35,000-square-foot former warehouse space in the Bywater, was originally supposed to be used as a space for a six-month show for Odums. Now it is a permanent art gallery, creative space, and classroom representing what Odums believes are the possibilities of radical imagination, when the artist conceptualizes something that is in front of them and sees beyond the present.

Studio Be – emphasis on the word "be" – which, according to Operational Manager Liz LeFrere, is about being in the moment and being present, is not a standard space. Odums, who has a penchant for painting in non-traditional spaces, fills the area with floor-to-ceiling murals on Sheetrock and physical walls as well as canvas, depicting Black culture in New Orleans and Black cultural leaders and icons. There are four "bays" in the space. Bay One is the Ephemeral Room, which is a visual conversation about Odums' relationship with time and how ephemeral moments from history inform where society is now and where it will go in the future. Bay Two is the Love Room which reflects on the various types of love: paternal, maternal, romantic, and platonic. Bay Three is for collaborative group shows, and Bay Four is a creative studio and classroom space. There is also a gift shop that sells original art, prints, and apparel.

With the success of Studio Be, in 2020, the team created Eternal Seeds, a nonprofit that helps young and emerging artists become revolutionary leaders and culture bearers who equitably benefit from their gifts. LeFrere, who is also the Director of Programs for the nonprofit, states it is their "commitment to our next generation of artists" to give them the tools and resources needed to sustain themselves and their models of expression, and ultimately manifest their own radical imaginations.

Address 2941 Royal Street, New Orleans, LA 70117 | Hours Wed–Sat 11am–6pm, Sun 2–6pm | Tip The Terrance Osborne Gallery on Magazine Street is a gallery that houses vibrant New Orleans art by its namesake artist.

103 Train Garden

Right on track for a good time

In a corner of the Botanical Garden, underneath a canopy of live oaks and crepe myrtles, you will find various New Orleans neighborhoods, multiple houses, and iconic landmarks all at 1/32 scale.

The layout at the Historic New Orleans Train Garden represents everything from iconic buildings such as Jean Lafitte's Bar, the Napoleon House, St. Louis Cathedral, and the Pontchartrain Beach Lighthouse, in miniature. The Audubon Zoo is featured and, although to scale, the gorillas and lions mingle with dinosaurs.

What started as a temporary installation for the park's 2004 Celebration in the Oaks festival, created by Applied Imagination (a firm that specializes in botanical architecture), became a permanent exhibit. When Hurricane Katrina struck in August 2005, it flooded just below the layout deck and in the building where its miniatures were stored. Train Master Bob Fairbank worked with multiple volunteers to rebuild, clean, and reassemble the Train Garden. Groups from across the country donated plants, and the garden was running again by Thanksgiving 2005.

The Train Garden can run up to eight trains on four tracks with a total of about 1,500 feet of track, or nine scale miles. The garden is divided up by neighborhoods in the 1940s, each with its own plants, buildings, and people. The layout is 485 feet, or three scale miles. There are also two St. Charles Streetcar lines, one West End streetcar line, and a Canal/Cemeteries Streetcar line. Placards around the garden supply information about the neighborhood as well as some of the famous buildings. Much of New Orleans' architecture is on display with shotgun houses, Greek Revivals, bungalows, Creole cottages, Queen Anne-style buildings, and Creole and American townhouses.

The Train Garden doesn't just connect the tracks to a model of New Orleans. It connects generations of those seeking a level of nostalgia, wonderment, and admiration for those whose artistic vision looms large through the creative details – even in miniature.

Address Botanical Garden, 5 Victory Avenue, New Orleans, LA 70119 | Hours Tue–Thu 10am–4:30pm, Fri–Sun 10am–4pm; trains only run on the weekend | Tip Mike's Train Shop in Kenner specializes in hobby model trains and remote-controlled toys, such as helicopters and airplanes.

104_Trixie's Burlesque Boutique

A one-stop shop for sparkle

Trixie's Burlesque Boutique is the sparkly mecca at the end of the sequined road for all things burlesque in New Orleans. Home to everything "naughty, bawdy, and gaudy," the boutique features glitter, pasties, vintage costumes, corsets, and handmade jewelry and headdresses. It is also a supporter of local and international artists (many pieces for sale are made by performers who had to pivot during the pandemic), an information hub for local shows, and a performance classroom.

On Easter 2022, the reigning Queen of New Orleans Burlesque, Trixie Minx, and her business partner, Emily Conelly, opened their one-stop shop for burlesque. This was not new territory for the popular performer. Trixie Minx Productions is the longest-running burlesque company in New Orleans. Aside from a variety of pop-up shows, the company has four regular shows that range from the traditional tease with a live jazz band to a variety show that features everything from drag queens and "boylesque," to aerialists, musicians, and singers. The boutique enables the burlesque curious and the burlesque enthusiast alike to have a personal experience with the art of the tease. Featuring a private classroom, students can learn from a burlesque performer such signature moves as the Bump & Grind, Shimmy & Shake, and the Sexy Strut with feathers and boas. Often, the classes consist of a group of women celebrating a birthday or bachelorette party, or sometimes, it is a solo customer wishing to surprise their partner with a striptease. "Many people want the experience but don't necessarily want to perform," Ms. Minx states, "so there's no striptease required; it's more about learning about movement and finding your sensuality."

You can experience all things burlesque at this boutique of glitzy inclusivity: buy a handmade fan, scan the store's QR code for local shows, or learn to shimmy. Just don't forget to take a selfie with Sophie II, the boutique's glamourous mannequin and "Patron Saint of Sparkle."

Address See website for current address: www.trixiesboutique.com | Hours Thu–Sun 11am–5pm | Tip Sparkles are a way of life in New Orleans, but if you are celebrating your birthday, be sure and pin a dollar bill on your shirt. Locals will wish you happy birthday, pin money on you, and occasionally buy you drinks!

105 Tulane Special Collections

The magic of Mardi Gras

Tulane University Special Collections (TUSC) is a treasure trove for those interested in Louisiana and New Orleans history. The holdings consist of almost 2,500 archival items, more than 100,000 volumes of rare books, some dating back to the 13th century, and other remarkable materials that detail the history of New Orleans and beyond. The collections include everything from the Louisiana Menu and Restaurant Collection to the Gettysburg letters of Confederate General Robert E. Lee, and the complete archives of famed novelist Anne Rice, including her personal diaries, photographs, correspondence, and hundreds of handwritten and typescript drafts of novels and poetry.

One of the prides of the TUSC archives is that it has the largest assortment of original Carnival float and costume designs predating World War II, which is considered the golden age of Carnival. The TUSC has almost 6,000 of these stunningly beautiful original watercolors depicting individual floats and riders. Today, some of the krewes (organizations) have over 3,500 members who ride in the parade and typically all wear the same costume and mask. In contrast, in the late 19th and early 20th centuries, each float would have five or six riders (compared to the 30 to 80 riders today), and each rider would have a costume specifically designed for them, giving a total of 100 to 120 unique costumes based on the krewe's theme for that year. Leon Miller, curator of the Louisiana Research Collection, equates the parades with street theater, where each rider performs as a specific character. Parade themes may have been devoted to different planets, different mythologies, and different cultures, all portrayed with a sense of beauty and wonder, and often exposing New Orleans to a wider sensibility.

Nothing can compare to viewing these exquisite pieces of art in person, but Tulane has recently put this entire collection online, allowing anyone, no matter where they are, to share in the magic of Mardi Gras.

Address 6801 Freret Street, New Orleans, LA 70118 | Hours Mon–Fri 8:30am–4pm | Tip The Boot, a no-frills bar located on the edge of Tulane's campus, has been "the place where your college career begins and ends" since 1965.

106_Twin Caryatids

Dual beauties

These massive twin caryatid statues have journeyed all over New Orleans. They used to have the spotlight of controversy shining on them, but now they are relegated to "blink and you will miss them" status.

The loosely draped, bare-breasted women each hold one hand to their head and the other their drapery. They used to stand guard in front of the New Orleans Cotton Exchange in the Central Business District, one of the most ornate structures in the city. At the exchange's pinnacle, one-third of the cotton production in the United States went through New Orleans, and the exchange sought to provide a centralized trading office. When the building was torn down in 1920, the caryatids (along with "sister statues" representing Agriculture, Peace, and Industry) were brought to City Park.

The caryatids were erected at the entrance to the park on Lelong Avenue, and the sister statues were erected near the Alexander Street entrance. Apparently, it was one thing to have half-naked 18-foot women greeting cotton traders, it was quite another to have them greet nature lovers. After complaints from offended "do-gooders," the caryatids were taken down. One architect called them "grotesque" and "junk," and said that City Park should not be used as a dumping ground. The sister statues were also removed.

The caryatids were later erected in front of architect and sculptor Albert Weiblen's company Weiblen Marble Works on City Park Avenue, where they stand today. The sister statues were placed in the back of Metairie Cemetery, where they were destroyed over the years by vandals and eventually became scrap.

The building has changed ownership and purpose over the years, but today, the solemn, bare-breasted and weather-worn women are barely noticed on busy City Park Avenue as they cast their perpetual gaze across the street at Greenwood Cemetery.

Address 116 City Park Avenue, New Orleans, LA 70119 | Tip The cemetery-dense area of City Park and Canal Boulevard has multiple cemeteries worth visiting. Centrally located is the Morning Call Coffee Stand, a place to get beignets and coffee before you start exploring.

107_The Unknown Enslaved

On holy ground

It is said that St. Augustine's Church is the only church where you wear your dancing shoes for service. The church is the oldest African American Catholic parish church in the US, which is fitting as it is in the historic neighborhood of the Treme, one of the oldest African American neighborhoods in the country. The Treme was one of the few areas during slavery where free people of color, Haitian refugees, and the enslaved who had purchased their own freedom were allowed to buy property. A few months before the church's official dedication in October 1842, free people of color began to purchase pews for their families. Upon hearing of this, white New Orleanians started to buy pews of their own. Thus, the War of the Pews was ignited, with the free people of color ultimately being triumphant, purchasing three pews to each one purchased by the white churchgoers. In a stunning move, the free people of color also purchased two outer rows of pews and gifted them to the enslaved as their exclusive place to worship. This resulted in one of the most racially and socially mixed congregations in the country.

One hundred sixty-two years after the church's dedication, the parishioners erected a shrine comprised of rusty grave crosses, chains, and metal shackles. The shrine is dedicated not only to the memory of the unknown Africans who died in the Treme but also to all the enslaved buried in the United States, particularly those in unmarked and unknown graves. To this day, human remains are still found in the immediate area. A plaque near the shrine reads: *There is no doubt that the campus of St. Augustine Church sits astride the blood, sweat, tears, and some of the mortal remains of unknown slaves from Africa…* The shrine was donated by Sylvia Barker, daughter of jazz musician, historian, and cultural bearer Danny Barker and singer Blue Lu Barker. It serves as a reminder that in this historic neighborhood, which has survived slavery, the Civil War, Jim Crow, and Hurricane Katrina, almost every step is on holy ground.

Address 1020 Henriette Delille Street, New Orleans, LA 70116 | Tip The New Orleans African American Museum is located just down the street at 1418 Governor Nicholls Street. It has rotating exhibits, musical performances, and an outdoor sculpture park.

108 The Voodoo Spiritual Temple

Awakenings

Born in 1943 in Mississippi, Voodoo Priestess Miriam Chamani made her way to New Orleans via Chicago, where she studied spiritual and occult work. After years of preaching, she was ordained a Bishop at the Angel Angel All Nations Spiritual Church.

Originally, she and her husband, Priest Oswan Chamani, planned to live in Belize, but after a series of serendipitous events, they ended up in New Orleans in 1990. The couple worked in the Voodoo Museum, establishing their own temple, the Voodoo Spiritual Temple (VST), shortly after. Priest Oswan passed in 1995, and Priestess Miriam preserves their work, which focuses on helping people resolve their personal crises and bringing resolution to life's problems.

Toward the end of 1998, a Simbi spiritual guide, in the form of a mermaid, appeared to Priestess Miriam in a dream and told her to prepare for a long journey. The mermaid reappeared in early 1999 and told her to "put a book in her pants and hold on tight." The mermaid and the priestess "swished" through the sea and resurfaced on foreign shores. Less than 10 months later, Priestess Miriam was on a flight to Russia to teach Voodoo to a collection of citizens who were unable to obtain information on the religion. She spent three weeks instructing, giving readings, and performing rituals.

Priestess Miriam continues her work at the VST, specializing in spiritual guidance and consultations, including African bone castings. She sells mojo bags, her own line of essential oil blends, and handcrafted spiritual bags. Her temple is filled with what Priestess Miriam describes as "hitchhikers," a sundry collection of items that have made their way to her through various means and people such as porcelain dolls of Princess Diana and Pope John II, a St. Theresa statue, African and Indonesian masks and statues, drums, and rum. The vast collection represents the life of a woman who has existed on many platforms.

Address 1428 N. Rampart Street, New Orleans, LA 70116 | Hours Mon–Sat 10:30am–6pm | Tip Baldwin & Co. is a Black-owned bookstore and community hub named after James Baldwin, and is known for its carefully curated selection of literature, coffee, and local events.

109__Whitney Plantation

Where Gone with the Wind is gone

If you want a bucolic plantation tour with guides in hoop skirts describing the sleepy days of Antebellum life under a trellis of Confederate jasmine, this is not the tour for you. Located 35 miles west of New Orleans, the Whitney Plantation is the first nonprofit museum in the country dedicated to the history of slavery.

The plantation was founded by German immigrant Ambroise Heidel in the 1750s as an indigo farm. Over the years, the family adapted and altered the spelling and pronunciation of their name to Haydel as well as changing their crop to sugarcane, which was a back-breaking crop to process, and often tantamount to a death sentence.

After the Civil War, the plantation was sold to Bradish Johnson, who named it Whitney after his daughter. For over 100 years, it remained a working plantation with workers and overseers. It was sold in the 1970s to be turned into a heavy industrial site. The plans never came to fruition, and in 1999, self-made New Orleanian John Cummings purchased a portion of it. Upon learning its history and admitting to his own naïvety on the topic, he spent over 15 years turning the plantation into an educational experience.

The property has original historic buildings (including weathered cypress cabins and a jail), but what is most poignant is its endeavor to give a voice and reverence to the enslaved. Several memorials occupy the grounds, including various statues, a granite wall engraved with the names of the 107,000 enslaved who lived in Louisiana before 1820, and a "Wall of Honor" with the names of the 354 enslaved who worked on the property. A graphic memorial exists to the German Coast Uprising in 1811, when approximately 95 enslaved revolted and were ultimately killed. Dozens were decapitated and their heads placed on spikes as a warning to others enslaved. Also sobering are the clay statues by Woodrow Nash of enslaved children placed throughout the grounds. The Whitney Plantation takes you on an experience that is highly emotional and often unsparing.

Address 5099 LA-18, Edgard, LA 70049 | Hours Wed–Mon 9:30am–4:30pm | Tip The Angela King Gallery on Royal Street, in the French Quarter, sells Woodrow Nash's sculptures.

110 Yvonne LaFleur

Elegance without pretense

Shopping at Yvonne LaFleur's namesake store is not an excursion; it is an experience. LaFleur, who opened her shop in 1969, is a trained seamstress and renowned custom milliner. She offers her own lines of apparel (casual and couture) and carefully handpicks the other items. From the moment you step into the 10,000-square-foot shop, your posture straightens and you're transported back to a time when refinement was standard. Hats are everywhere, from felt or fur cloches trimmed with antique feathers from Germany to wide-brimmed straw hats adorned with silk ribbons from Switzerland and turn-of-the-century silk flowers from France.

LaFleur says that the modern Southern lady changes outfits multiple times during the day and has an "after-five wardrobe." All can be found on LaFleur's racks and shelves: casual wrap dresses, business suits, beaded evening bags, cashmere capes trimmed in fox, silk stockings, chiffon bodice dresses with jeweled belts and feather skirts, and various styles of gloves displayed in an antique case. From brunch to ball to bridal (there's a separate boutique in the back), nowhere else will you find dresses appropriate for "Mother of the Queen" or "the King's Wife." And if necessary, the store alters everything on-site for free.

Despite the abundance of elegance, there is not an ounce of pretense to be found. LaFleur's knowledgeable staff is not only trained in wardrobe design, but also keeps customers' favorite champagnes and wines on hand. Gentlemen can wait at the fully stocked 72-foot-long bar nestled between the scarves and the gift-wrapping station. All of LaFleur's wrapping is decorated in violets (as is her signature perfume). LaFleur says that violets represent loyalty, something she not only inspires in her customers (many are third generation) but also demonstrates herself. As fellow designer Coco Chanel once said, "A girl should be two things: classy and fabulous." She can achieve both at Yvonne LaFleur.

Address 8131 Hampson Street, New Orleans, LA 70118 | Hours Mon–Sat 10am–6pm | Tip If you're looking for some shoes to match your latest Yvonne LaFleur ensemble, the family-owned and operated Feet First is the city's largest independent shoe and accessories retailer.

111__ZIP NOLA

The world's only swamp zipline

While there are multiple swamp tours offered on airboats, pontoon boats, and even some with cushioned seats and restrooms, Zip NOLA is the only fully aquatic zipline in the world where one can get a bird's-eye view of the swamp. Located a half mile off of the 112,615-acre Maurepas Swamp, Zip NOLA is just 30 minutes outside of New Orleans and offers a distinctive experience for nature and adventure lovers alike.

There are five platforms, all built around bald cypress trees, the highest being 65 feet. The average zipline trip takes between 10 to 15 seconds. The enthusiastic guides demonstrate various tricks such as the "starfish" and "deadman," slowly building up the level of difficulty at each platform and factoring in the speed, height, and length. For safety reasons, guests are always between one of the guides. "A lot of people who come are nervous or scared," says guide Giovanni Dionisio, "and we have the ability to empower people to conquer their fears."

The swamp below holds racoons, nutria, deer, turtles, white egrets, and of course, the main attraction – alligators. Ask the guides to point out some of their favorite alligators, many of which have names. Stumpy, who is missing the end of his tail; Winky, who is missing an eye; Diablo, who has a gash down his back and is known for being a bit feisty; and Richard, a nine-foot gator with a mellow personality, who according to the guides, just looks like a Richard. The guides often work around the swamp inhabitants instead of the other way around and sometimes find hawks' nests or racoons who decided to invoke squatters' rights on one of the platforms, but this is always handled respectfully with the guides never seeming to lose their awe and reverence for nature.

The average experience takes between an hour to an hour and a half, and Zip NOLA offers transportation to and from multiple hotels in New Orleans, giving people the opportunity to experience two unique types of wildlife: the wildlife of Bourbon Street and the wildlife of the swamp. For many, the latter is much less wild.

Address 301 Peavine Road, Laplace, LA 70068 | Hours Daily 9am–6pm | Tip Maurepas Swamp also offers a ½-mile-long nature trail, located on the east side of U.S. Highway 51, approximately a ½ mile north of Peavine Road in LaPlace.

1
51
Lake Pontchartrain
113
111
West End
Lakeshore
Spanish Fort
Lakeview
10
10
Kenner
Metairie
61
61
55
Faubourg St. John
90
Mid-City
Hollygrove
5
French
Quarter
Elmwood
90
NEW ORLEANS
Broadmoor
Harahan
Mississippi River
90
Greenville
Uptown
Garden District
4
Waggaman
90
Westwego
3
Marrero
Harvey
N
0
0.8 mi
Lake Cataouatche

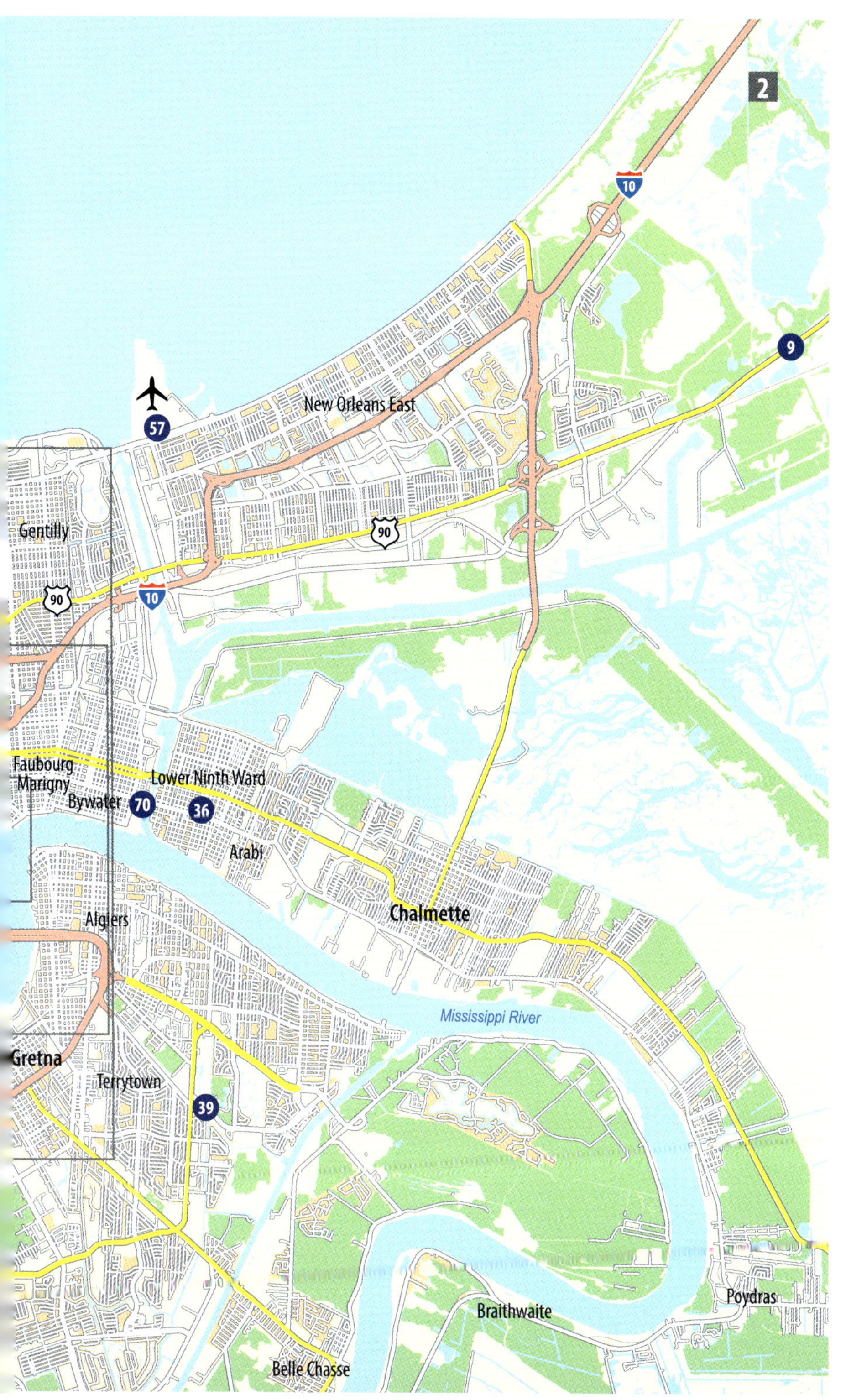
2
10
9
57
New Orleans East
Gentilly
90
90
10
Faubourg
Marigny
Lower Ninth Ward
Bywater
70
36
Arabi
Algiers
Chalmette
Mississippi River
Gretna
Terrytown
39
Braithwaite
Poydras
Belle Chasse

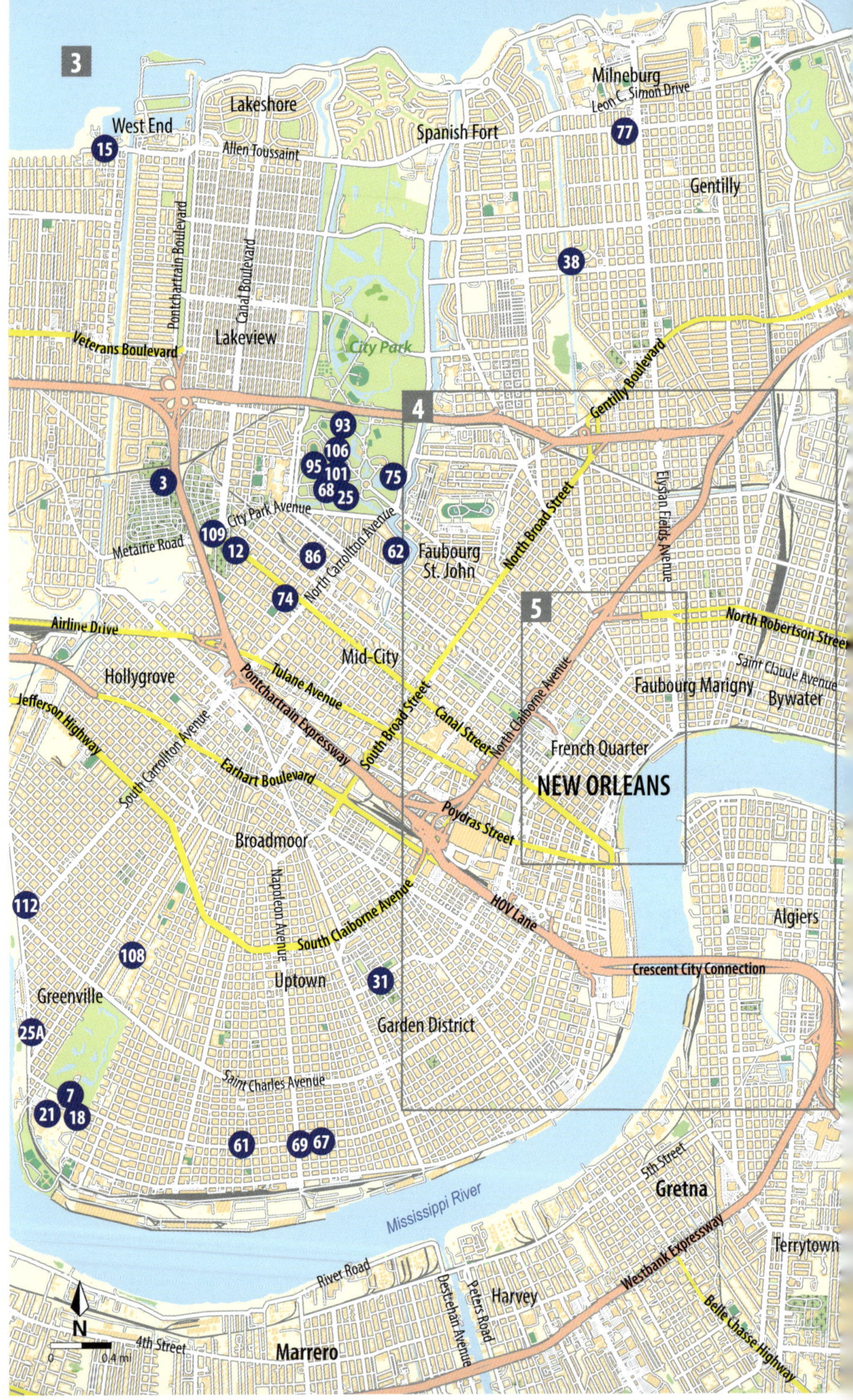
3
West End
Lakeshore
Allen Toussaint
Spanish Fort
Milneburg
Leon C. Simon Drive
Gentilly
Pontchartrain Boulevard
Canal Boulevard
Lakeview
Veterans Boulevard
City Park
Gentilly Boulevard
4
City Park Avenue
Metairie Road
North Carrollton Avenue
Faubourg
St. John
North Broad Street
Elysian Fields Avenue
5
North Robertson Street
Airline Drive
Mid-City
Saint Claude Avenue
Hollygrove
Tulane Avenue
Pontchartrain Expressway
South Broad Street
Canal Street
North Claiborne Avenue
Faubourg Marigny
Bywater
Jefferson Highway
South Carrollton Avenue
Earhart Boulevard
French Quarter
NEW ORLEANS
Poydras Street
Broadmoor
Napoleon Avenue
South Claiborne Avenue
HOV Lane
Algiers
Crescent City Connection
Uptown
Greenville
Garden District
Saint Charles Avenue
5th Street
Gretna
Mississippi River
Terrytown
River Road
Westbank Expressway
Destrehan Avenue
Peters Road
Harvey
Belle Chasse Highway
N
0
0.4 mi
4th Street
Marrero
15
77
38
93
106
95
101
68
25
75
3
109
12
86
62
74
112
108
31
25A
7
21
18
61
69
67

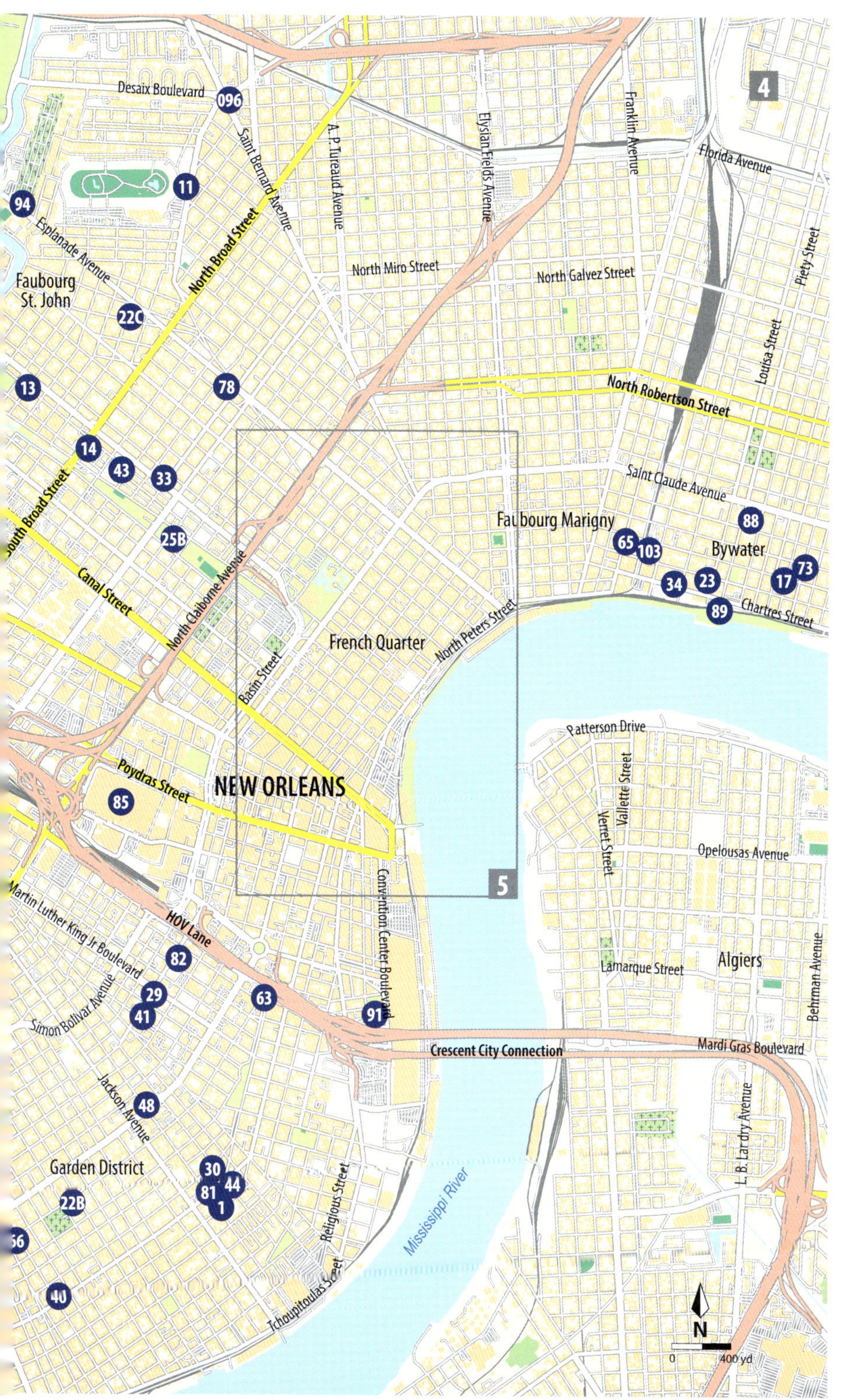

4
Desaix Boulevard
096
Saint Bernard Avenue
A. P. Tureaud Avenue
Elysian Fields Avenue
Franklin Avenue
Florida Avenue
Piety Street
94
11
Esplanade Avenue
North Broad Street
North Miro Street
North Galvez Street
Faubourg St. John
22C
Louisa Street
13
78
North Robertson Street
14
43
33
Saint Claude Avenue
South Broad Street
25B
Faubourg Marigny
88
65
103
Bywater
Canal Street
North Claiborne Avenue
34
23
17
73
89
Chartres Street
French Quarter
North Peters Street
Basin Street
Patterson Drive
Poydras Street
NEW ORLEANS
85
Vallette Street
Verret Street
Opelousas Avenue
5
Convention Center Boulevard
Martin Luther King Jr Boulevard
HOV Lane
82
Lamarque Street
Algiers
Behrman Avenue
29
63
41
Simon Bolivar Avenue
91
Crescent City Connection
Mardi Gras Boulevard
Jackson Avenue
48
L. B. Landry Avenue
Garden District
30
44
81
1
22B
Religious Street
Mississippi River
66
40
Tchoupitoulas Street
N
0
400 yd

5
97
Urquhart Street
Marais Street
Bayou Road
Kerlerec Street
84
North Prieur St.
Ursulines Avenue
Henriette DeLille
52
Tremé
110
8
Barracks Street
Esplanade Avenue
45
Saint Philip Street
Governor Nicholls Street
105
Royal Street
28
Louis Armstrong Park
North Rampart Street
20
Burgundy Street
St Philip St
Bourbon Street
Royal Street
58
53
64
Decatur Street
North Peters Street
22A
37
100
79
French Quarter
French Market
St Peter Street
107
99
27
Storyville
47
92
24
72
60
83
102
Basin Street
Jackson Square
4
Conti Street
71
10
49
87
Canal Street
Royal Street
59
Common Street
NEW ORLEANS
Mississippi River
O'Keefe Avenue
16
6
2
Central Business District
Carondelet Street
South Peters Street
Convention Center Boulevard
80
Fulton Street
76

Dana DuTerroil, Joni Fincham, Daniel Jackson
111 Places in Houston That You Must Not Miss
ISBN 978-3-7408-2265-1

Dana DuTerroil, Joni Fincham, Sara S. Murphy
111 Places for Kids in Houston That You Must Not Miss
ISBN 978-3-7408-2267-5

Kelsey Roslin, Nic Yeager, Jesse Pitzler
111 Places in Austin That You Must Not Miss
ISBN 978-3-7408-1642-1

Travis Swann Taylor
111 Places in Atlanta That You Must Not Miss
ISBN 978-3-7408-1887-6

Gordon Streisand, Alex Streisand
111 Places in Miami and the Keys That You Must Not Miss
ISBN 978-3-7408-2403-7

Susan Veness, Simon Veness, Kayla Smith
111 Places in Orlando That You Must Not Miss
ISBN 978-3-7408-1900-2

Cristyle Egitto, Jakob Takos
111 Places in Palm Beach That You Must Not Miss
ISBN 978-3-7408-2398-6

John Tucker, Ashley Tucker
111 Places in Richmond That You Must Not Miss
ISBN 978-3-7408-2653-6

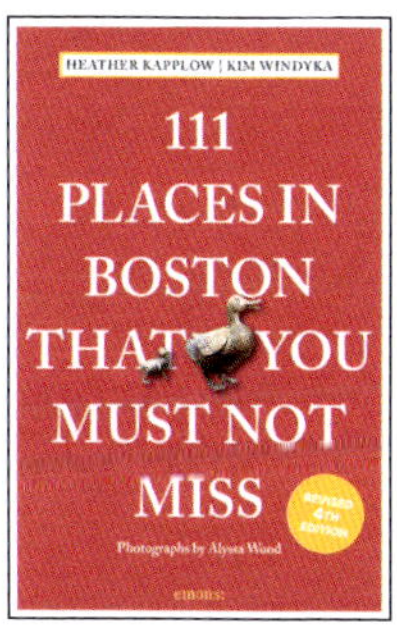

Kim Windyka, Heather Kapplow, Alyssa Wood
111 Places in Boston That You Must Not Miss
ISBN 978-3-7408-2655-0

Jo-Anne Elikann, Susan Lusk
111 Places in New York That You Must Not Miss
ISBN 978-3-7408-2400-6

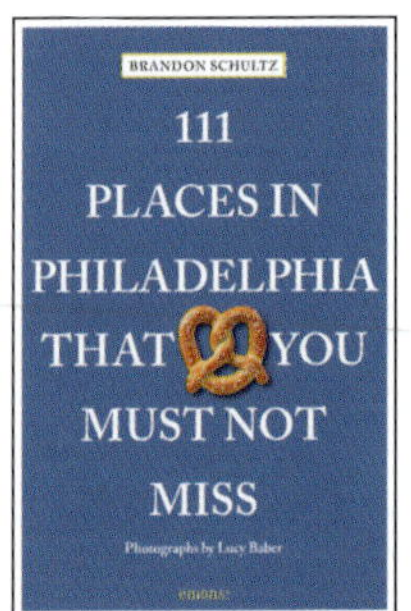

Brandon Schultz, Lucy Baber
111 Places in Philadelphia That You Must Not Miss
ISBN 978-3-7408-1376-5

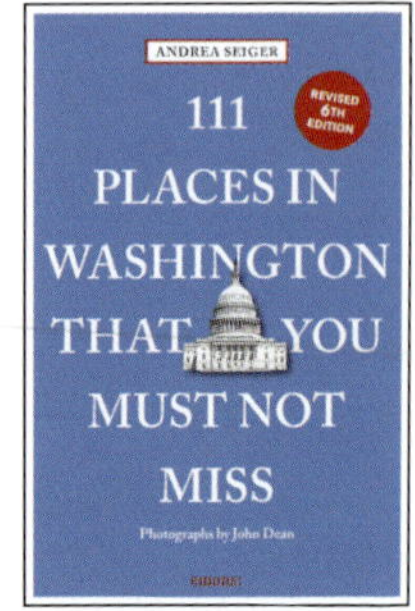

Andrea Seiger, John Dean
111 Places in Washington That You Must Not Miss
ISBN 978-3-7408-2656-7

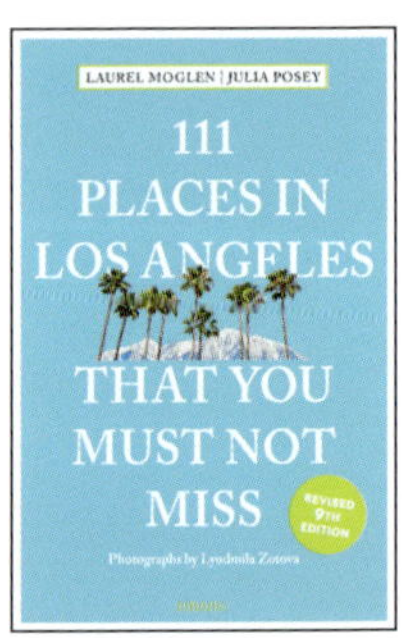

Laurel Moglen, Julia Posey, Lyudmila Zotova
111 Places in Los Angeles That You Must Not Miss
ISBN 978-3-7408-2573-7

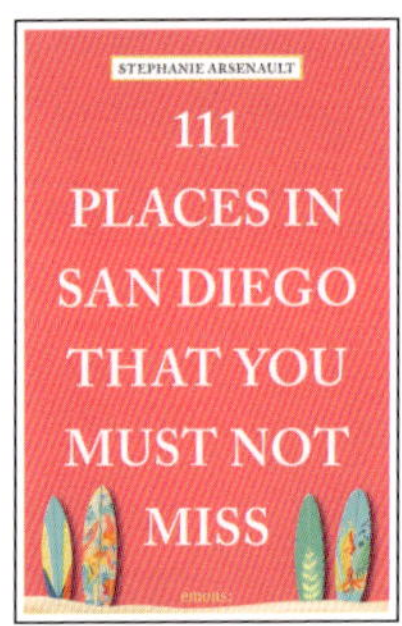

Stephanie Arsenault
111 Places in San Diego That You Must Not Miss
ISBN 978-3-7408-1540-0

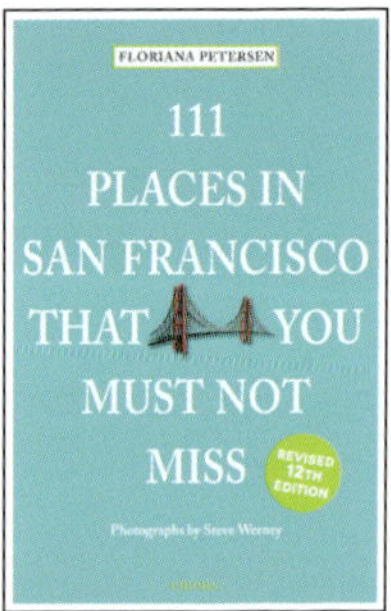

Floriana Petersen, Steve Werney
111 Places in San Francisco That You Must Not Miss
ISBN 978-3-7408-2058-9

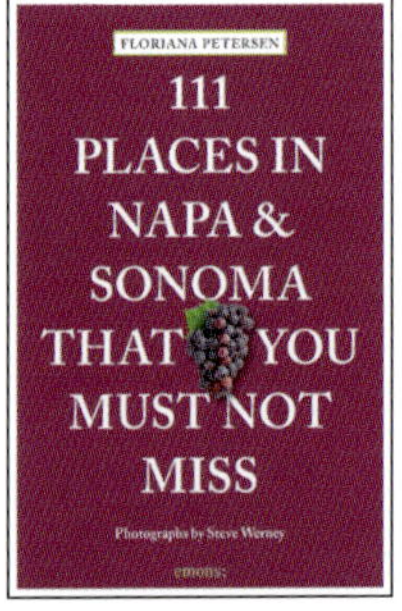

Floriana Petersen, Steve Werney
111 Places in Napa and Sonoma That You Must Not Miss
ISBN 978-3-7408-1553-0

Travis Swann Taylor
111 Places in Phoenix That You Must Not Miss
ISBN 978-3-7408-2050-3

Philip D. Armour, Susie Inverso
111 Places in Denver That You Must Not Miss
ISBN 978-3-7408-1220-1

Acknowledgements

Thank you to my editors Karen Seiger, Tania Taylor, and Laura Olk for their patience and guidance. Thank you to Jen Blakeslee, Katy "Trixie" Hobgood, and Chelsea Christopher for their unwavering support.

Special recognition and thanks need to go to Poppy Tooker, who is not only an amazing cheerleader but was instrumental in helping me make connections.

Thank you to all my friends who modeled for me and to all my friends who volunteered to model for me. Thank you to the artists, performers, business owners, museum curators, and specialists who took the time to talk with me and answer my questions. You keep this city hummin'!

Of course, extra special thanks must go to my "team," Huckleberry Button Asher, Zuzu Bisou Asher, and Ava Dauphine May. I could not have done it without you. And thank you, New Orleans, you never cease to surprise and amaze me. I love you.

Sally Asher is a New Orleans-based author and photographer whose work has appeared in such publications as *Newsweek, The New York Times, U.S. News & World Report*, and *New Orleans Magazine.* She owns and operates her own tour company, Red Sash Tour, which specializes in authentic cultural New Orleans tours. Asher is a former president of the nonprofit Save Our Cemeteries and is on the board of the Preservation Resource Center. She is a proud member of the Crescent City Oddfellows #73 and is involved in many Mardi Gras krewes. Asher lectures about New Orleans' history in various venues throughout the city and state. This is her fifth book about New Orleans.